OLD NOTTINGHAMSHIRE REMEMBERED

Keith Taylor

Published by Sigma Leisure – an imprint of
Sigma Press, 1 South Oak Lane, Wilmslow, Cheshire SK9 6AR, England.

British Library Cataloguing in Publication Data
A CIP record for this book is available from the British Library.

ISBN: 1-85058-372-2

Typesetting and Design by: Sigma Press, Wilmslow, Cheshire.

Front Cover: Mr Meates and Mr Anderson, two Wollaton Park employess with the horse-drawn 'Greens' mowing machine. (Photograph: F. Parkes)

Printed by: Manchester Free Press

Preface

For me, the seeds of local history were sown a little before I was five years old due to the fact that like most of their generation, my parents loved walking. And just as they had wandered the woods and fields of a gradually extending city boundary during their early days together, so they took my sister and myself on rambles throughout the summer weekends and evenings of the last war.

As the first occupants of a house on Chalfont Drive, Western Boulevard, we were soon made aware of a choice of directions; by standing at the front gate and, looking east, we saw the factory-etched outlines of Radford and the city beyond contrasting with the remnants of Shepherd's Wood, with its trees frequently etched into the burnished splendours of the sunset to the west. Between the last house on Chalfont Drive and Shepherd's Wood was a tract of land that had once been farmed as part of Lord Middleton's estate. Flanking those forgotten fields a broad stony track, known locally as Colliers Pad, terminated on the left side of Chalfont Drive but continued between cattle grazed fields and through a wilderness of derelict allotments in the direction of Aspley Lane under the more summer-enriched name of Cherry Orchard.

There were many such Cherry Orchards in the English lowlands at that time and just as many Bluebell Woods, I suppose. Perhaps they too brought poignant memories to people who are in their seventies and eighties today, for the Cherry Orchard of which I write was to linger in the minds of couples who married before the war and moved away from the area; some to different towns; others to countries on the other side of the world. But it was my own generation who used its wild unmanaged acres as a mysterious forest, nature reserve and battlefield where, as children, we made dens, re-enacted scenes from black and white films, floated tin baths in flooded ditches, gathered berries and occasionally found a bird's nest.

This evocative stretch of countryside that extended north-east of Wollaton Hall to the bordering hedgerows of Aspley Lane was overlooked by the tower of St Margaret's Church which we regarded as being the next point of civilisation. As we played our games, one or other of us would sometimes stumble across the remains of an old pram or a table screened by elder and raspberry thicket. We also came across the occasional small pile of house bricks surrounded by stinging nettles.

Later in the day, we usually returned to the spot carrying spades and garden forks. The term 'treasure trove' was mentioned several times as we approached our make-believe castaways' island. And so we dug and the treasures we unearthed usually comprised of several minute toy cars, a few tin or lead soldiers and a small doll or two – usually with a limb missing.

The culmination of these local explorations occurred on the Sunday afternoon that I was taken by my father to Shepherd's Wood. We had watched hares racing through the meadow grass and heard several cuckoos calling from tree branches obscured by foliage. But it was deep into this sylvan and secretive place, divided by a narrow clearwater stream, that I experienced a sense of excitement when I saw a great pile of house bricks partially overgrown with grass, ivy and bracken fronds, rising like an island from within a sea of dead nettles.

I have since learnt that nettles are an indication of human or animal habitation. Yet, although I was not aware of this in my formative years, the mossy mountain of house bricks conveyed the same message to my enquiring mind.

Someone had actually lived here in the middle of the wood. But who? And why in the middle of a wood? I suspect that I plagued my father with these questions on the homeward route down Beechdale Road which represented little more than a single track thoroughfare, with ragwort flowering from the cracks in its uneven surface.

When next I met my friends, I told them of my exciting discovery and added that one day I would find out who had lived in the Shepherd's Wood house. By the following day, though, I had already forgotten the matter in the way that children do.

In the early sixties, when Colliers Pad had been transformed into the road and pavement of Redbourne Drive, the correspondence columns of the evening newspaper resurrected Cherry Orchard for people living as far apart as Radford and New Zealand. Letters written in America and Australia were also featured, with paragraphs describing forgotten past times like 'flappin gaffs' or grey-hound races, pitching the horseshoe, and picnicking beneath near idyllic skies.

A field called 'Humps and Hollows' was mentioned in conjunction with memories of gathering cowslips and collecting plover eggs. Courting couples had frequented certain favourite dells and they knew them almost as well as the local poachers had known the hedgerow gaps used by rabbits, hares, pheasants and partridges. Cherry Orchard was also etched firmly in the mind of Nottingham-born author Alan Sillitoe, and commemorated within the pages of his distinguished work 'Raw Material', as was the nearby mining community of Radford Woodhouse and the row of cottages that, for some curious reason, were known collectively as Engine Town. Colliers Pad was also mentioned in Sillitoe's book of short stories, entitled *The Loneliness Of The Long Distance Runner*.

Some forty years after I had walked by the mound of bricks in Shepherd's Wood, I was talking to Lionel Baker who, by then, held the position of Superintendent of Wollaton Park. I had known Lionel for about thirty years and we usually conversed whenever our paths crossed, but he had never mentioned his boyhood years; nor had I asked him about them until someone happened to mention the fact that he had lived at Cherry Orchard, near Aspley Hall Farm and St Margaret's Church.

It was around this time that I decided to make notes about the different ways of life and the comparisons which could be made between present times and sixty or seventy years ago. I found Lionel to be both a colourful and cooperative raconteur as he recalled his boyhood spent in the house that was situated in the middle of Shepherd's Wood. Obviously, the house had fallen into disrepair by the time I came upon the scene and was probably pulled down at the bidding of the Middletons' land agents soon after the plots were sold off by auction in the 1920s.

When, eventually, I began putting my pen to the paper with Lionel sitting across from me and rebuilding the house and its memories within his mind, it seemed as if the seed of my interest in local history had begun to germinate after having remained dormant for those forty-odd years.

Enthused at the realisation that other recollections could also be gleaned by talking to the elderly, I struck up conversations with the few I met while wandering the fields, woods and footpaths of my county and the many I spoke with while visiting various rest-homes in Wollaton, Nuthall and West Bridgford. Some of the interviews I have relayed almost exactly as they were related to me but others, due to such difficulties as the lack of time, I have used vignette fashion with the intention of producing a background scene.

In a volume of this size it is impossible to cover every part of the county, but what I have attempted to do is portray the people I have met as the individuals they so obviously were.

On a final note, I would like to thank and acknowledge the support of people who have allowed me the privilege of publishing some aspects of their lives – including the few who were very cooperative but wished to remain anonymous. I also extend my thanks to the librarians and staff of the Local Studies

Department who took the trouble to advise me on locations, maps and suggested various photographs.

AUTHOR'S NOTE

The Author wishes to acknowledge the fact that, at the time of going to press, the people interviewed in the pages of this book had each given consent for their names and past or present locations to be mentioned.

Keith Taylor, Wollaton

Contents

THE BAKERS OF CHERRY ORCHARD

The fields and woods featured in this chapter were once situated within the square of land that lies just north of Wollaton Hall. Today, this is regarded as a wholly built-up area bordered by Wollaton Road, Western Boulevard, Aspley Lane and Robins Wood Road.

Beechdale Road could perhaps serve as an adequate dividing line; but, in the days of which I write, the track that led north from Beechdale Road to Cherry Orchard and Aspley Lane was for many years known as Colliers Pad until it was widened in the early sixties to become a thoroughfare with houses, bungalows and maisonettes built on either side.

Thus, this last existing stretch of footpath that the colliers had walked daily from their homes in Basford to the colliery at Wollaton was widened, laid over with tarmacadam and given the more formal name of Redbourne Drive.

In the days when the Bakers lived in Shepherds Wood, the 'Humps and Hollows' field mentioned in the introduction, was by-passed on the left as one walked along Colliers Pad in the direction of Aspley Lane. On their forays to Engine Town and Radford Woodhouse the Baker children often used a path that crossed several fields. Today the Government Buildings occupy the site that was once ploughed in readiness for the corn harvest and grazed by the cattle of Aspley Hall Farm.

From a wide drainage ditch on the left side of Colliers Pad rose an elm tree of immense height and stature. Fortunately, this same tree was still towering skywards when I was a boy living with my parents on Chalfont Drive. The right-hand side of the path nurtured a high hawthorn hedge beyond which were strewn a mass of elder and hawthorn thickets.

Here, in the autumn, we filled jam jars with wild-growing blackberries and raspberries but I believe these derelict allotments were still being cultivated during the years that the Bakers were living at the house in Shepherds Wood.

Where Colliers Pad met with pavements of Chalfont Drive the roots of another elm had found secure anchorage in the sides of the ditch. Known locally as Three Nail Tree, its boughs offered a challenge to adventurous boys and youths who frequently dangled from strong ropes and swung from a considerable height with little thought, of what would have happened if the rope had snapped and they had been plunged to the ground.

At this point, the track became Cherry Orchard, shadowed by high hawthorn hedgerows and more derelict allotment on the right-hand side but with fields, still extending across to Shepherds Wood on the left.

If we were to take this route today, we could do it only by walking along the right-hand pavement of Trentham Drive, imagining perhaps the scene as it appeared in the early forties, with a long field of ploughland beyond the hedge on the left and the trees of several fine spinneys surrounding the white house and red pantiled outbuildings of Aspley Hall Farm clustered below the tower of St Margaret's church.

Where the long field ended, a stile allowed the walker access across two splendid meadows grazed by breeds of cattle that are rarely seen in the countryside of present times. But it was on these buttercup-swathed meadows that I was taught how to differentiate between a Dairy Shorthorn, Red Polled, Ayrshire and Blue Albion cow long before I found the inclination to chant out the twelve-times table in the classroom at the Whitemoor Infants School, Basford.

Cherry Orchard's allotment wilderness also terminated at the stile. From there, until the boundary hedgerows met with the pavement of Aspley Lane, the New Aspley Gardens attracted the retired men who were keen to sell their home grown fruit and vegetables and displayed hand made notices in front of their rickety allotment gates to this effect.

Bordering the Cherry Orchard path beyond the stile a high, wrought iron fence separated the grazing cattle from the pedestrian way. This fence continued along until the field came to the edge of Aspley Lane.

Some quite magnificent Scots pine and horse chestnut trees surrounded Aspley Hall Farm. On fine autumn mornings these attracted 'nutting parties' in from as far afield as Cinderhill and Bestwood as George Bramley relates in a further chapter. If we were to turn left when we reached the end of Trentham Drive and walk in the direction of Bilborough and Strelley, there are still a few houses and cottages that look almost the same as they did sixty or seventy years ago. The vicarage has retained much of its serene atmosphere surrounded as it is by pine trees, lawns and rose gardens. The neat, red bricked farmworkers' cottages appear as smart and clean-cut as they did in the days of my boyhood.

Aspley Hall Farm was reached by walking a few hundred yards along the lane with the outbuildings, stables and stockyards on the left and a field below the well trimmed hawthorn hedgerow opposite. In the summer months this lane was shielded by an avenue of elm and lime trees.

The Hall farmhouse gleamed white in both sunshine and rain. Its individualistic splendour was further highlighted by the doors, window frames and shutters which were painted pale blue. The lawns and shrubberies surrounding the house always looked immaculate as did the carefully swept gravel drive leading up to the front door. On the west side of the farmhouse, a cluster of cart and carriage sheds were dwarfed by the bulk of a Dutch barn in which stocks of hay were stored to provide winter fodder for the dairy herd.

The south windows overlooked acres of parkland pasture inset with several spinneys. In the summer these spinneys provided islands of shade for the cattle that grazed the seemingly endless carpet of grass and buttercups.

The cattle also herded into the field that lay between the Dutch barn and the sturdy post and rail fence of Aspley Lane. To look into this field, a boy had to run swiftly up a steep bank and clamber around the craggy remains of seven decrepit elm trees. These, my mother explained, were known as The Seven Sisters.

Today, most, if not all, of this area is under concrete or topsoil. Little exists to endorse the fact that a fine manor house and farm had been built there and rather than give the new roads and crescents such names as Aspley Hall Close or Seven Sisters Crescent, the housing complex is known as Eskdale Drive, a name that has little significance in keeping with both bygone times and the present locality.

Over the Beechdale Road side of the estate however Hollington Road was carved out of the fields around the outbreak of the Second World War and named after the Hollington family who, like the Bakers, lived in an isolated cottage, but closer to Horseshoe Wood.

Mr Hollington, as the head of the family was known, was employed as stockman to the tenants of Aspley Hall. Had we continued walking up Aspley Lane those seventy or eighty years ago we would have eventually reached the slender footpath over which Robins Wood Road has since been laid.

This original path took the walker by the coverts of Robins Wood and on into Shepherds Wood where we would have seen two houses blocking the sun-dappled glades.

In one of these houses lived 'Humpy' Wilson the Aspley Hall gamekeeper and his wife. The second was occupied by a family of boisterous happy children, their parents and grandfather.

Should we have been bold enough to have knocked on the door, we would most probably have been asked inside the house the moment it was opened and introduced to the members of the family, who were known collectively throughout the parish as The Bakers of Cherry Orchard.

Lionel Baker was three years old when the family moved from the Lincolnshire hamlet of Byards Leap to the equally isolated house in Shepherds Wood, situated west of the Nottingham border and about two miles from the Wollaton Hall estate. Lionel's father had found employment with the firm of timber merchants R.F.R. and W. Brown who ran the business from beside the lane which crossed the railway and canal between Aspley and Wollaton.

Employees at Brown's Sawmills, Woodyard Lane, Wollaton. Among them are Dennis Milward, Arthur Lamb, Harry Tucker and two Polish refugees. (Photograph: A.Winters)

This rutted thoroughfare, though perhaps three quarters of a mile in length, was known first as Brown's Woodyard and later, Woodyard Lane. Today the still narrow link road has been given the name of Lambourne Drive. The main timber yard was situated on the left between the canal towpath and the foreman's cottage and offices as one walked the lane toward Wollaton Road. Further along, and screened by horse chestnut trees, carts pulled by horses and steam engines towing larger carts were assembled in a large walled yard and the consignments of timber loaded or unloaded accordingly.

Where the lane dipped slightly to the left, a grain store, harness shop, row of stables, blacksmith's forge and farrier's cabin opened out directly onto the cobbled surface and faced a garden of some two or three acres which was situated on the right.

Partially hidden by ornamental fir trees, Scots pine and laurel bushes was the spacious house called The Lawns, which is standing to this day although a housing complex called Splean Court has been built on most of the garden and looks out onto the main Nottingham – Wollaton road.

At 'The Lawns', some seventy or eighty years ago, lived the Brown families and their small staff consisting of a butler, housekeeper, several maids and cleaner.

Lionel's father however spent his first few years in the main timber-yard and during that time his large, young family were kept busy exploring the house and the surrounding woodland glades in which they lived. The Bakers' house comprised six bedrooms, three downstairs rooms, a large kitchen and huge cellar. Next to the house was a small yard with a water pump and shed where Mrs Baker carried out her weekly washing chores.

The other sheds were always called 'Grandad's Sheds' for here the senior member of the family kept his garden tools, axes, saws, grindstone and billhooks. In another shed Grandad Baker repaired the family's boots and shoes and, if there was plenty of cooking and washing to keep Lionel's mother occupied, there was also a never-ending row of worn boots for Grandad to be cobbling because, in all, the Baker children numbered nine boys and three girls.

Although he was living about eighty miles away from his natal Lincolnshire hamlet Grandad Baker repeatedly told the children how Byards Leap got its name but, although they had heard it many times, they were also keen to hear yet again the story about the gallant knight, who on his charger named Byard, rode into the hamlet with the intention of ridding the district of a terrorising witch.

One day when the knight was riding close to the lane side the witch appeared and stuck her long claw like nails into the side of the old war-horse with such force that he leapt high into the air and came down so heavily on the other side of the lane that his hoof prints stayed engraved within the turf for the next few hundred years. In fact when the Bakers were moving house four large stones were still marking the legendary descending place of the knight's gallant charger. But Lionel recalls there being little time for much story-telling when he was young for the children were kept busy from dawn until dusk.

Each night, before it was badly needed, the boys around home would be sent through the glades or out along the edge of the wood to collect kindling. Sometimes small arguments would break out about whose turn it was to go. But always there would be three or four members of the family detailed to collect kindle for without it no kettle could be boiled on the hob the following morning and no water could be heated for the family to take it in turns to soak in the big copper bath placed beside the hearth. Once it was collected, all the kindling was stacked into the oven to keep it warm and dry in readiness for use the following day.

But enjoyable were the mornings when Lionel would go to collect the eggs of the hens, that were locked up each night in a shed filled with straw and intriguing the minutes spent crouching in the half gloom with his brother Les, who would sit and talk to a hen if he thought she was about to lay and induce her to produce the egg much quicker.

"If anybody can persuade a hen to lay an egg, it's our Les," Lionel's mother used to say to the people who visited the house. Beside collecting eggs, Lionel learnt to milk a cow grazing out on the open pasture before anyone at Aspley Hall Farm realised what he was about. A little later in the morning he, or one of his brothers, would carry a pail up to the farm and collect the family's daily allowance of milk with a look of innocence on his face that made the stockman smile and gently ruffle the lad's hair if he happens to be standing close by.

One morning, Lionel was leaving the wood by ducking between two strands of barbed wire with the milk pail in one hand, when, to his astonishment, he saw what he thought was a bull thundering across the field towards him. Hastily, he retreated inside the wire fence then when the polled grazer turned broadside he realised his mistake for the 'bull' had swollen udders. Without further hesitation he scrambled back into the field delighted at having made acquaintance with Aspley Hall's pet 'house cow' and from that day took advantage of her services with bold regularity.

One autumn day, Lionel's milk delivery service was held up when he stopped to watch the hounds and huntsmen assembling at Aspley Hall for an infrequent day's foxhunting. The few marauding foxes that entered the three estate woods were usually accounted for by the Baker's gamekeeper neighbour whose main task was to rear pheasants, by the hundreds, for the visiting gentry to shoot.

The farmer, George Taylor, was generous in many ways and in the early autumn kept the Baker family supplied with apples, pears, plums and damsons grown in the nearby orchards.

Sides of salted bacon were regularly hung from the beams and rafters of the old house and it was also in the autumn, that Grandad Baker would put his shoe repairing chores aside and concentrate on making pork pies and home made wines in readiness for the darker days ahead.

The highlights of the Baker children's country year were, of course, provided by those days spent picnicking in the hay-making fields, helping to position the stooks and leading the cart-horses home to the farm. Lionel recalls the winter days being long when he was too young to be attending school. But still he tramped around in the snow beneath lowering skies, collecting kindling, searching the sheds for hens' eggs, taking the pail to the farm and bringing back the ration of milk and throwing snowballs for Queenie, the family's cross-bred collie, to chase after.

Childhood games included 'goose and stick' in which one ordinary stick was hit with the end of a pointed stick so that the former bounced into the air. (But to what ends, neither Lionel nor myself have the faintest idea.)

Another game was whip and top. Lionel remembers the tough, gaudily-painted 'window breaker' tops which, once a certain skill had been acquired by their handlers, could be sent spinning off at a surprisingly colourful tangent.

A more secretive pastime, when the weather permitted, was using a leaf-filled sack suspended from a tree branch as a punch bag, but once the Baker boys tired of this they indulged in bouts of all in wrestling, then trudged home with their clothes askew and muddied much to their mother's annoyance.

There dawned another day when Lionel and his brothers were able to explore the fields on the far side of the wood, for word had got around that several seams of opencast coal had been discovered.

"Some of us carried a bucket in each hand. Others had shovels, bowls and all kinds of contraptions to carry the coal in and we didn't go home until we were well and truly loaded down with it," Lionel explained when I visited his home. Though fuel found by collecting dry branches, boughs and twigs was very much on the minds of the less-fortunate folk living in those times the warmer days of spring and summer brought a welcomed diversion into their lives although kindling still needed to be collected.

With their father teaching his sons how to identify one tree species from another, Lionel soon learned that the Shepherds and Horseshoe Woods consisted largely of elm, ash, oak, larch and spruce.

Primroses and violets were embedded firmly within the woodland glades and along the hedge banks. Profusions of cowslip and buttercup studded the fields with carpets of yellow. In May the glades were massed with bluebells and the thickly foliaged tree branches hid the loftily calling cuckoo and drumming woodpecker.

Lionel loved to look for bird nests; but he never took the eggs. He just enjoyed looking at the exquisite fashionings of the chaffinches deep cup and the domed security interpreted by the plush, rounded fortresses of the wren and long tailed tit. Bluebells were picked and picnics laid out on the 'Humps and Hollows' field overlooked by the towering elm which both Lionel and I have known throughout the bridging span of time that divides our years.

Eventually, most of the Baker boys got the knack of marking the spot where courting couples were laying out in the grass. Lionel, in particular, recalls one evening spent sitting on the fence until the lovers left then going to the flattened hollow and as usual putting his fingers through the grass blades in his search for the odd coin or two that may have dropped from the man's pocket. That evening, however, his fingers closed around a gold sovereign but he could not take it. Instead he ran towards the man who on having checked his pockets and discovered his loss was making his way back to the spot.

Lionel quickly intercepted him, explaining that he had seen the coin gleaming in the sunlight and gone over to investigate. Much to his surprise the man thanked him emphatically then strolled back to the spinney where his lady was waiting in the shadow of the elms.

When he was old enough to attend school in Wollaton village, Lionel walked the two miles each morning with his brothers and sisters. The route they took was by way of the western corner of Shepherds Wood and then along a rough track across the fields to Woodyard Lane.

The rough track was, for some long forgotten reason, called Dobs No Lane. Long since hidden by houses and gardens it would have lain somewhere close to the road now known as Freemount Drive.

The pleasant walk along Woodyard Lane I also savoured as a boy although I used it to reach the canal or the entrance gates to Wollaton Park beyond, unlike Lionel who with his mischievous brothers and sisters sometimes ran and sometimes walked along its uneven surface which led up between the fields to the high bricked railway bridge and then downhill to the farmhouse on the right.

The road continued over the canal bridge with Browns Wood on the right and the timber stacks of Browns Sawmills on the left.

It then swung by the foreman's house and loading yards to the corner buildings where the blacksmith worked at the anvil. The gardens of the old house called 'The Lawns' stretched the entire length of the hedgerow on the right and beyond the wrought iron gates Lionel occasionally glimpsed the gardeners mowing the lawns or tending the shrubberies.

Facing the house on the left-hand side were the carters' sheds and stables. A cluster of workmen's cottages was set back in the fields where the lane joined

Wollaton Road. The village was situated about three quarters of a mile further along the road. To reach it the children walked alongside the Wollaton Park wall and up the tree-shaded hill by the church. This proved to have been an extremely interesting stretch of road for the Baker children. Frequently they looked over the wall and saw the estate workers putting up a fence or sawing the boughs of a tree.

Or sometimes they lingered on the top of the wall watching the cattle, red deer and fallow deer grazing across the forty-acre field that fronted the slopes on which Wollaton Hall was built.

Lionel admits to having occasionally rung the gate bell at Lodge Two and earned the wrath of tenant Jack Lane when he opened the lodge gate to admit a visitor but saw instead a crowd of chuckling schoolchildren running up the road towards the village. When the rooks were nesting in the oak and ash trees high above Jack Lane's lodge, the Baker children loved to clap their hands or bang a stick against the wall in their efforts to send the birds up from the tree branches in a great swirling and a cawing crowd.

The schoolhouse, a few yards down Noggins Lane (called Bramcote Lane today) was managed by a very strict headmaster who was known to his pupils as 'Gaffer' Jordan. He was the only male teacher in the establishment and he married the only female teacher. Thus, the Baker children had little difficulty in remembering the names of both their teachers. The basic lessons were arithmetic, reading, writing and spelling. But Mrs Jordan occasionally allowed the girls to play basketball or hockey and her husband encouraged the boys to excel in games of football and cricket.

During the light evenings the Baker children searched the hedgerows close to home with the hope of discovering the first violets of the year. They watched the red squirrels running nimbly along the tops of the post and rail fences and away into the wood. They also admired the magnificent beds of daffodils thriving in the grounds of Aspley Hall and occasionally, if there was no one around, Lionel and his brothers or sisters would take a hurriedly-picked bunch of these flowers home to their mother.

Each child in a family of twelve could be expected to have two or three good school friends and on Sunday afternoon the Bakers' house in Shepherds Wood soon became the playground of several children from Wollaton village. Most of these children stayed for tea and the old homestead rang with riotous outbursts of laughter. Even the vicar at nearby St Margaret's church began to notice that the Sunday tea time gatherings were becoming a regular weekly occurrence, especially when Lionel and his friends walked over to the vicarage and asked if the family could borrow the couple of sizeable tea urns that were kept in the church hall.

The vicar granted their request but seldom, if ever, saw any of these young boys among his scant congregation. But in having anticipated that their children would be 'entertaining half of Wollaton every coming Sunday' Lionel's parents increased their grocer and greengrocery orders that were delivered from the few shops in Wollaton, Radford and Aspley.

Huge joints of meat were already being brought to the house by the local butcher's lad and it was the baker and confectioners happy task to deliver the bread and cakes three times a week.

Lionel remembers the days when it was not uncommon for fifteen loaves of bread to be delivered on a Monday and again on the Wednesday with a further twenty loaves filling the cupboard again by the last hour or two of Friday evening. But when the friends of the Baker children began to call so regularly the entire order for bread was increased to fifty-six loaves a week, about a dozen cakes and several bags filled with fairy cakes, jam tarts and cream horns.

Grandad Baker was by this time mastering the art of walking with a pair of crutches. But his mischievous grandsons began to tease him by putting soot from the fireplace onto the end of his nose when he had fallen asleep in his favourite armchair and attempted to suppress their laughter as they tied his bootlaces together. At this point in Lionel's story, I have quite often remarked that it was small wonder the old man was by then walking on crutches but in a way I suppose the Baker boys received their just deserts because, disabled or not, their grandfather had still to draw a small pension every Thursday from the post office on the main Nottingham -Ilkeston Road. To achieve this, he put each of his grandsons on a weekly rota, allowing them to play truant from school so that whichever boy's turn it was had to walk with him the three and a half miles to the post office and then of course, make the return journey.

Only Grandad Baker and his weekly escorts knew how long it took for a man on crutches to cover a distance of three and a half miles and because he was aware that either one of his young grandsons might become bored and go off in search of some beckoning boyhood adventure, the old man soon got the knack of looping a length of clothes line around his waist and that of the boy and away they would go across the fields, down by Engine Town and Radford Woodhouse, the boat builders' cabins and eventually to the canal bridge, where they turned left and journeyed a further one and three quarter miles to the post office.

There were days, usually in the early autumn, when the Baker's neighbour 'Humpy', Wilson shot the occasional red or fallow deer that had escaped from the walled confines of Wollaton Park.

Once he had bled the beast, the gamekeeper would tie a rope around its hind legs, suspend the body from a tree bough then walk the length of Woodyard Lane, with his shotgun tucked under his arm and dogs trotting at his heel, his intention being to call at one of the gate lodge entrances to the Wollaton Hall estate.

After conferring with a member of the staff he was eventually put in touch with a gamekeeper who harnessed a workhorse to a flat dray and accompanied by another man, who was needed to help lift the deer, the gamekeeper and Humpy would guide the conveyance back along Woodyard Lane to Shepherds Wood. Eventually, old Humpy called upon the Baker children and asked them if they would take on the role of beaters for the autumn pheasant shoots.

Once their interest had been confirmed the gamekeeper called again at the Bakers' House on the evening before each shoot to make arrangements with the boys and allocate the particular coverts he wanted them to work. Knowing that Lionel was an early riser, Humpy listed several coverts and stretches of woodland that he wanted the boy to survey. Closer to the actual time that the shoot was about to begin Lionel's next task was to walk around the periphery of the coverts and drive the outlying pheasants gently back into the thickets.

When Lionel was promoted to beater, he could either receive a cash payment for the several hours work that was involved or a brace of pheasants for the family's Sunday dinner. Consequently, if his several brothers each accepted a brace of pheasants there was enough game meat for everyone and perhaps just a little left for tea.

George Taylor, the tenant farmer of Aspley Hall invited such local notables as Loscoe Bradley and Jesse Boot (Lord Trent) to his pheasant shoots as well as the local newspaper proprietor Colonel Foreman. On very rare occasions the owner of the estate, Lord Middleton, also took part and among the subjects raised was always that concerning the fact all that the local estates were being ravaged by several gangs of poachers which were believed to have lived in and around Radford. In his attempts to thwart these poachers, 'Humpy' Wilson, and his predecessor Mr Thornton, frequently laid taut trip wires across many of the woodland glades and rides on the Aspley Hall estate.

The 'cock cock' calls of pheasants going to roost in the tree branches were familiar sounds to every member of the Baker family. But if a stranger was seen crossing the fields between the Shepherds and Horseshoe Woods he was immediately regarded with suspicion and apprehended by the gamekeeper as quickly as possible. Nor was he allowed to forget the fact that he was walking over private land.

One early autumn morning, Lionel's mother glanced up from her kitchen chores and saw their gamekeeper neighbour crawling up the grass ride on all fours. When she went out to investigate the ashen faced man was unable to speak but a long trail of blood began darkening the grass over which he was crawling.

In her efforts to get him into his house, she propped open the front garden gate, ran up the path to the front door and summoned the keeper's wife. Together the two women helped the stricken man into a fireside chair where they bathed and bandaged the very deep wound in his neck.

When the gamekeeper recovered from the shock and was able to speak without undue effort they learned that he had been cutting down bramble tendrils with a billhook and lifted his hand so high that the blade had bitten into his flesh. Fortunately the gamekeeper recovered sufficiently to recommence his duties.

It was still dark when the Baker children set off for school in the depths of winter. On the way there and on the journey home the blacksmith's forge in Woodyard Lane lured them across to warm their hands and the blacksmith would talk to them while he continued to hammer and shape out the irons for the horseshoes. Often Lionel, or one of his brothers, would ask the man if he knew where their father had been sent that day, for Mr Baker was by then employed as the driver of a Browns timber wagon, and the blacksmith would often name a place that the children had never heard of but might well be doing in the years to come.

In the darkness of a winter night, gas lights from the two houses partially screened by the bare branched trees of the woods would glow and appear as two small golden yellow circles as the children walked the last stretch of Woodyard Lane. When finally they opened the door, leaving the wind and rain to the night, fires piled high with coal and kindle would be roaring up both the kitchen and dining room chimneys and the children lost no time in drawing the curtains across the windows.

To provide the boys with some form of recreation during their long winter nights, Lionel and his older brothers used to soak flattened sections of wood from a felled elm in a tub of water then round off the edges with tools borrowed from their father's kit-bag. They would then skilfully divide the board into sections and by the end of a week had made their own dartboard. The darts, I believe, they bought from a shop in Radford.

At bedtime, Lionel or his brothers carried a Kelly lamp up the stairs or if someone had taken a lamp up before them they had to make do with a lighted candle.

As one can imagine, Christmas was a crowded, exuberant and a colourful affair with streamers, log fires, homemade wines, fruit, game, poultry, vegetables in continual supply throughout the relatively short holiday period. On the festive morning, the children came downstairs to see presents, colour wrapped and stacked around the foot of a tree which had been brought in from the nursery gardens of the Aspley or Wollaton Hall estate.

When fuel was running low Lionel's father would visit the estate steward and seek the landlord's permission to fell an aged tree. Just occasionally this request was met by a firm refusal which incited the Bakers into felling a tree whether the landlord favoured the action or not.

First Mr Baker would cross to the far side of the wood and select his source of fresh timber, then return to the house and instruct his sons to filter out into the woods along different paths at different times. This done they stood around while their father felled the tree then helped him split off the boughs and branches to each of which he would attach ropes and have the boys drag home.

The axe-whitened tree stump they would hide from the gamekeeper's gaze by covering it with lengths of grass and briar and rubbing soil or mud over the stump's outer surface. Running the gauntlet of their gamekeeper neighbour the boys hid the tree boughs and branches in the thickets and coverts throughout the daylight hours then when the night had settled across the fields they returned and furtively dragged the timber home, evening by evening perhaps over the period of a week and stored it all in the outhouses where it dried off before being split into smaller logs and chippings needed for these two welcoming fires.

When winter passed and the skylarks began to sing above the fields that wonderful sense of freedom returned but as they neared the thirteen or fourteenth birthdays the Baker boys set their sights beyond Three Nail Tree and the 'Humps and Hollows' field, for their appetites had been wetted by the glimpses they had gained of community life around the streets of Radford Woodhouse. And it was in that direction that their thoughts began to turn.

WANDERINGS AROUND RADFORD WOODHOUSE

Much to his delight Lionel discovered that his father had decided to draw up a rota which gave each of his sons an insight of life beyond the woods and fields of their Cherry Orchard House. This rota allowed a boy to play truant from school for a week at a time and during that week his task was basically to ride at the rear of the timber wagon driven by his father.

The timber wagon was pulled by a vehicle that resembled a small steam engine complete with funnel, flywheel and internal boiler. The name printed in bold letterings on the side of the wagon was that of 'R.F.R. and W. Brown, Timber Manufacturers'

The job of the boy riding the rear box, was to pull a cord when he saw a tramcar coming down the track so that his father could turn his load to one side of the tram tracks along which they normally travelled. For each day spent travelling with his father the boy was paid the princely sum of two shillings and sixpence. When his week of truancy arrived Lionel would leave Browns Woodyard in the early morning and travel to a destination they might not reach until the following day. The homeward trip would begin on the third day. Nights were usually spent in the bedroom of a public house and Lionel still speaks fondly of the pub lunches and suppers which consisted of little more than bread and cheese cobs washed down with lemonade.

The Browns were contracted to fell timber in various woods, forests and country estates throughout the English Midlands so that Lionel's trips took him out to Twyford Forest or the Browns original country home of Norton Disley. Occasionally his father was also instructed to fetch timber from Lord Middletons estate which was of course, Wollaton Park.

Many of the woodmen with whom Lionel and his father came into contact, talked mostly about the size and magnificence of the trees they had recently felled, and the characters, the gamekeepers, poachers and 'men of the road' they had met while on their travels. Most woodsmen lived in vardos or gypsy caravans, the interiors of which smelt strongly of the paraffin they used for heating while travelling between Wollaton and wherever they were due to stay over for the night. They pulled in whenever they happened upon a canteen or waggoner's café, where for a half-penny one could buy a scalding hot mug of tea and a plate filled with currant buns. In these rowdy establishments Lionel always experienced that sense of being in very genial company.

It was on those first outings with his father that Lionel became acquainted with the carter's café based on the main Nottingham – Ilkeston road at Radford. Everyone knew the café proprietor as Jack which was obviously the way the man intended things should be because alongside a wall poster advertising Wills Woodbine Cigarettes was a sign bearing the words

'tis the carter's café
Run by Jack
whose cakes and goods
No bad points lack

Jack apparently had a well-remembered sense of humour, for on another wall hung a rather ornate clock with a broken face. Beneath it was a slogan which informed the customer that there was 'No tic here'. Tic was, of course, a term commonly used in those days for any form of credit facility.

Once, when it was Lionel's turn to be the 'tram lookout' on the timber wagon the boiler plug blew from the steam engine just as they were a short way past Jack's café and the engine careered downhill completely out of control, and with Mr Baker sweating and labouring at the wheel. But to no avail, for the great battering ram on wheels crashed straight into the display windows of a butcher's shop. Fortunately, no one was hurt, but as Lionel put it to me ''there was glass and threats and curses flying in every direction.''

At weekends Lionel, with his brothers Fred and Loll (Lawrence) set off across the fields to the colliers' community at Radford Woodhouse, for they were growing up and unwittingly searching for new experiences. These they found among the youths and young girls who lived in the three streets of terraced houses which backed on to the railway line and could only be reached by walking Radford Bridge Road. There were ninety-eight houses in this community plus a chapel and corner shop which sold 'everything but the kitchen sink'. Three quarters of the way up one street was a haulier's business owned by Albert Tomlinson.

The Baker boys were warmly welcomed by the youths of their own age who were eager to visit the house in Shepherds Wood. So there was an interchange of environments between the two groups: "the country lads" and "the colliers' sons". Even 'Humpy' Wilson welcomed the new arrivals especially when they offered to make snares to help to keep down the rabbit population. Rabbit pie had appeared as regularly on the collier's dinner table as elsewhere but, once the gamekeeper had given them permission to set snares along the known rabbit runs and enter their ferrets into one or two of the big warrens, the Radford Woodhouse youths took dead rabbits across the fields each time they returned home.

Loll Baker told me that if one mining family failed to provide a home for a caged singing canary then they either had a couple of ferrets in a backyard or an improvised pigeon loft, with a roof of galvanised steel, taking up most of the back yard.

Rat baiting was another popular pastime. Brown rats were about the fields, streets and railway embankments in small legions. Most of the colliers sons caught them in caged traps, tipped the trap in the sack which they carried into a garden shed then, with their friends looking on, released the rat from the sack at almost the same time as they let a straining, trembling terrier into their midst.

On the 'Humps and Hollows' field, the lads played cards with serious intent. Not infrequently the local bobby on the beat would wheel his bicycle over the grass and check the hollows to ensure that there was no gambling taking place. When the lads were taken by surprise however, they grabbed their jackets, cards and coins and ran in various directions so that the poor constable could never really decide which one to pursue.

"But if he caught you he'd give you a bat around the ear and that would be it. There'd be no court case laid out or anything like that," said Lionel.

On hot summer evenings, and again at the weekends, all the youths would meet and walk across the fields to the canal towpath. The locks and pounds between Lenton and Wollaton numbered fourteen in all, therefore the watermen's term 'The Wollaton Flight' was a correct application to the immediate terraces.

One lovely stretch of canal near 'The Roughs' was bordered by silver birch thickets until, in the Baker boys' time, the colliery began dumping mountains of slag and slurry over the vegetation and it became buried beneath a series of ugly grey mountains.

But despite the inevitable eyesore, the surrounding countryside was still beautiful and the colliery standing beside the canal pound and the slag heaps were regarded as an essential asset to the industrial and occupational scene. Here, where the colliery chimneys were partly reflected across the canal's surface the water entering from the industrial outflow was contrastingly warm, therefore, hardly a fine evening passed that failed to see the likes of the Baker boys and their friends donning their swimming trunks and diving in from the lock gates, as they followed the example of their fathers and grandfathers who had swam the curved canal pound known locally as 'The Hotties' but which more gentile folk preferred to call 'The Warm Waters'.

Some weekend mornings after several enthusiasts had released their racing pigeons along the railway embankment, or from the wild growing acres of the Humps and Hollows field, the youths used to take their collections of disused horseshoes to the fields and indulge in prolonged bouts of the game called pitch and toss.

Later in the day they would receive word about whether some members of the mining community had decided to stage a 'flappin gaff'. 'Flappin gaffs' were unofficial whippet races where bets were accepted and rough tracks were laid out. Some whippets were so swift that they helped raise their owners social position within the local community. Some whippet owners were so keen on showing off their charges that they insisted on staging several practice days before the main event.

It was, of course, important that the local bobby on the beat be lured across to the far side of the parish before a flappin gaff actually took place, and when this had been arranged then the colliers and their whippets assembled on the 'Humps and Hollows' field in no uncertain manner.

Bets were placed and each owner would restraint his whippet until the 'starter' dropped his white handkerchief. The winners were treated with the utmost respect while the owner of a continual loser was looked upon with an air of contempt. Lionel remembers a particular whippet coming in next to last in every race. Its owner was abashed. "This dog's a bloody waste of time and energy" he frequently bemoaned.

Eventually, however, plans were afoot to drown the poor unsuspecting creature in the canal, but when it came to actually putting a rope around its neck and attaching this to a brick' or lump of concrete to keep it secured to the canal bed, none of the men, for all their boastfulness, could do it.

But the mood of irritation soon passed especially when a friend of Lionel's nudged the whippet's owner and murmured: "Are you still having trouble with that whippet of yours?" "Of course I am", the whippet's owner replied.

"Well, I tell you what – let's all run off and leave it".

The sudden thought of three men trying to outrun a whippet brought hoots of laughter to the street, to such an extent that it became a standing joke among all the onlookers and whippet owners who entered their charges in for 'a flappin gaff' and, because of this, the slow dog's owner began to regard his animal in a more light-hearted way, although it was never entered into another race.

Both Lionel and Loll still loved to watch the blacksmith pounding out horse shoes on the anvil and when the knife grinder was on his rounds they would follow him until he paused to set up shop. "Line props. Your scissors and knives to grind" the man would shout sing-song fashion after which men, women and children came out of their houses clutching knives, scissors and anything that required sharpening, while the man fixed his grindstone to the pedal wheel attached to his bicycle.

"You could always rely on there being a goodly crowd of people standing around the knife grinder and a string of youths trotting in his wake for just as long as he was in the parish"

Lower down Radford Bridge Road on the right-hand side, if the walker is heading towards the Nottingham Ring Road, stands a white painted farmhouse which in Lionel's day was tenanted by working farmer, Jack Matthews.

Mute swan pair in reeds backing on to Jackie Matthews' farm, Radford Bridge Road.

His fields backed onto the canal bank and the land he farmed stretched from the back-water which came to the side of the road then followed the water course until it almost converged with the railway line passing beneath the bridge on

Woodyard Lane. It was not an extensive tract of farmland and Jack Matthews preferred arable to dairy farming, a decision which put a little money into Lionel's pocket, for with his brothers and the Radford Woodhouse youths, he was paid for working occasionally on the fields.

The boys all earned this part-time money by spending hours picking beans, peas and potatoes. One thankless task was that of following the farmer and dropping a cabbage seed in each on the many hundreds of holes his employer had dug or drilled along the furrows. They were allowed to snare rabbits for the pots but the few pheasants which tenanted the canal-side coverts were regarded as exclusive targets for the farmer's gun. Directly behind the farmhouse was a wharf where the bargees off-loaded sacks of lime for the kilns standing nearby on Jack Matthews land. Here between the towpath and the hedgerow a pair of mute swans built their sizeable nest and annually reared a brood of cygnets.

Jack Matthews' yard was used as a scratching ground by his many free-range hens. Occasionally the farmer also grazed a group of Emden Toulouse geese on a rough field alongside the house and also fed grain to his fleet of Khaki Campbell ducks which paddled, and dabbled, in the canal and sometimes nested in the hawthorn tangles some little distance from the farmyard.

But Lionel and his brothers were always aware of this and searching for duck eggs became a bonus that the farmer was never fully aware of although on one occasion, he refused to pay one of the Baker boys because he claimed the lad had been talking to his friend instead of picking potatoes.

The farmer, incidentally, admitted to having watched the part time workers through binoculars while standing at his bedroom window 'and if you talk you don't get paid' he declared and, like many of his kind, meant exactly what he said.

It was in the streets of Radford Woodhouse that Lionel first met Lucy Hardy, the girl he was eventually to marry. Ted Hardy was Lucy's father who like most of the local men worked on the coal face although at first glance one would hardly have taken Ted for a collier due to his slender build, quiet voice and neatly-clipped moustache.

I became a friend of Ted's myself, but much later, when he had retired from the pit and was working as a patrolman on Wollaton Park. Like several at that time in my life, his friendship was greatly treasured and the eventual news of his death struck me as deeply as it would had I received similar news regarding the death of my father. Lionel was of course a frequent and welcomed visitor to the Hardy household. He and Lucy met several evenings each week and to get to the Nottingham cinemas they had to walk across several fields and unlit lanes to catch a tram from Hartley Road to the centre.

The late Ted Hardy, retired Radford collier,
with his bull terrier 'Sall'

One foggy night, in the depths of winter, Lionel escorted Lucy home then set off to walk the familiar route across the fields to the isolated house in Shepherds Wood. The fog however was so thick that he became completely disorientated and after two attempts to cross the fields was forced to admit that he was lost on ground that he had been wandering over for the past thirteen or fourteen years. While relaying this incident, Lionel also told me that a person walking in fog always bears left instead of keeping straight ahead and this was obviously the reason why he twice struck out for home, along what he had come to regard as a familiar path, only to find himself much lower down the Shepherds Wood fence than he had originally intended. In fact he never reached the fence until after his third attempt during which time he fell into the hollows of the Humps and Hollows field and skinned both knees.

Eventually of course he managed to grope through the fog, the thickets, and the darkness to the welcoming door of the house which was by then lacking a little in fun and laughter because Grandad Baker had died and the children were growing up and going their various ways.

The winter of the knee skinning fog however was also the one in which Lionel befriended Jim Hollington, one of the sons of the Aspley Hall stockman, and on the night when he was not seeing Lucy he went around to the Hollington's isolated cottage close to Dobs No Lane and spent hours with Jim listening to his crystal set radio.

But each weekend the Baker Boys re-assembled for Saturday and Sunday afternoon games of football. This they played on a field close to the Wollaton Village Rectory and almost opposite the entrance gates of Lodge Two.

Most of the Baker brothers monopolised the local team and the pitch is remembered for being a sloping tract of ground with quite a sizeable quagmire forming the lower goal. During wet weather the leather football soon became soaked and heavy especially when the participants of the game had to dribble or kick it uphill and several local sages have assured me that a pitch of such calibre was destined to sort out 'the ninety-minute lads from the others'.

By this time many changes were taking place throughout the neigbourhood not the least of which was the sale of Wollaton Hall, the Elizabethan mansion house which had been the ancestral home of the Willoughby family and, in later years the Middletons.

The foundations of Wollaton Hall were laid in the year fifteen hundred and with the help of the world-renowned architect Robert Smythson, the entire structure was completed eight years later. Its walled parkland provided grazing for deer and cattle and eventually pheasants were reared in the woods and decoy ponds formed the swampy areas to attract wildfowl in as sport for the shooting gentry.

Lionel and the Baker boys however were born at the time when the Middle ton family had moved to more comfortable quarters at Birdsall in Yorkshire but retained a large staff to manage the affairs and maintenance of the Hall and its parklands until they were sold to the Nottingham Corporation for the sum of £200,000 on the 18th May 1925.

Rather than accept a humdrum routine offered by one of the many Nottingham factories Lionel sought the possibility of working at Browns Sawmills when he left school but eventually secured an interview with Messrs Render and Bell, who were acting as land-agents for the Wollaton estate, which resulted in him being taken on as an apprentice stonemason. However, Lionel because of his restless nature, discovered that remaining in one place more or less day after day was not quite for him and so he transferred to the gardening and estates staff, a team of men who were supervised by their kindly foreman, 'Father' Parkes.

Mr Parkes became the first superintendent of Wollaton to receive a wage packet from the Nottingham Corporation. Thus the entire staff became Corporation employees and, like many, Lionel remembers 'Father' Parkes as being the kindest man they have ever worked under. If he was approaching a blind corner and knew that his workers would eventually be in sight 'Father' Parkes used to whistle to let them know he was coming.' If he needed a packet of cigarettes fetching from the single shop in Wollaton Village, he would send Lionel or another young man, but not before he had been to every man present with a notepad and pencil at the ready and asked if there was any particular item that they also required from the shop.

'Father' Parkes had worked at both Sandringham and Stoneleigh before coming to Wollaton and so his horticultural experience, coupled with his thoughtfulness, won him the respect that any man in his position could expect.

So it was under the eye of this gentleman that Lionel first patrolled the avenues and paddocks of Wollaton Park and picked up any litter that might have been thrown down by the public after the gates of the country estate had been opened to admit the people of Nottingham on a permanent basis.

Another of his duties involved walking in a straight line before a workhorse harnessed and pulling a grass mowing machine and picking up any branches or stones that may have chipped the cutter blades had they not been removed.

At the outbreak of the last war Lionel enlisted for service with the Royal Air Force and served abroad. He was eventually promoted to the rank of corporal.

On his demobilisation the deep attachment he had always nurtured for his family, plus the prospect of young Lucy Hardy waiting at Radford Woodhouse were reason enough for him to return to Nottingham, where he was re-assigned to the Wollaton Park staff under the direction of Mr Frederic Hollows. By this time, 'Father' Parkes had retired and Lionel soon found himself among men whom he would know for the greater proportion of his working life.

Lawn maintenance and the propagation of plants and flowers appealed greatly to the country boy who married Lucy and for a time the couple lived in the turretted gate-house on Derby Road, known as Beeston Lodge. At night it was lit from the outside by a singular gas lamp. In the autumn Lionel sometimes heard the stags roaring as they crossed the bracken swathed slopes of Arbour Hill. There were still a few pheasants on the estate and small parties of these fine birds could occasionally be seen strutting across Derby Road to the rhododendron thickets bordering the grounds of what is now the University Campus. Tawny owls hooted from the oaks and pines, Red squirrels were also to be seen especially in the pines directly opposite Beeston Lodge for here the road swept in a wide bend towards Beeston and one of the A.A. patrolmen, who was on alternative duties there, took a keen interest in these animals and observed them at relatively close quarters. Lionel and Lucy were eventually allocated a council house on the then-new estate at Lenton Abbey which was no more than a five minute bicycle ride from Wollaton Park. Having settled in, the couple raised a family in the home they would share for just as long as they were together.

When Wollaton Park had been opened to the public for a few years, it was decided by the relevant committees that a patrol staff was needed to ensure that the rules and regulations were being carried out and such vandalism as might occur was kept down to a minimum. Consequently the Nottingham Estates Committee, who were responsible for the ground management of both Wollaton and Newstead Abbey, engaged a small team of retired policeman to enforce the regulations.

Throughout the 1950s, one such gentleman was George Glanville who lived close by on Orston Drive. Being sympathetic towards my interest in natural history, George never failed to inform me of the weekly wildlife sightings and occurrences at the park and it was due to our friendship that I first met Lionel Baker.

I was about fourteen years old and the September evening bore a noticeable drop in temperature that had George and me exploring the possibility of the red deer rut beginning earlier than usual. The unmistakable tang of decaying leaves was in the air and save for stutterings of a cock pheasant going up to roost the shadowy avenues of the parklands projected a strange, almost uncanny, stillness.

While walking my dog and, at the same time savouring the atmosphere of this early autumn dusk, I turned towards a plantation of Wellingtonia pines and saw George standing beside the fence, bicycle alongside and similarly enjoying the silence.

In less than a minute we were talking in low voices, when George looked beyond me and lifted his hand in greeting. I turned to see a bronzed and very fit looking young man wheeling a bicycle across the grass in our direction. He wore a russet, three-quarter length overcoat, grey hardwearing trousers and boots. His hair was dark brown and wavy. His smile indicating instant warmth and friendship.

George introduced him to me as Lionel Baker, the foreman gardener, and although the two spent quite some time discussing matters concerning the running of the park, I was occasionally brought into the conversation. For instance, I remember asking Lionel if he had ever found the cast antlers of a stag or fallow buck and he replied that the gardeners had been known to pick them up when they were collecting leaf mould in the woods.

As he spoke, I sensed that, so far as his occupation was concerned, Lionel was a contented man, a state of mind for which I soon became envious. In less than no time I had decided that I wanted to work outdoors, preferably in Wollaton Park, but when I left school the Careers Officer chose to ignore my request and gave me instead a list of shops and factories that were in need of junior employees. I next saw Lionel about a year later for he was one of several men herding cattle into a truck placed by the gateway of Middletons Paddock. This scene alone filled me with the awareness of how variable estate work can be and I became even more determined to somehow become involved with both land and livestock.

Just as the following years changed for myself so they changed for Lionel, but we both stopped for a word whenever there was a moment to spare, and by the 1960s he had succeeded Frederic Hallows as Park Superintendent.

Meanwhile, George Glanville had introduced me to his working partner, and Lionel's father-in-law, who with his wife and bull terrier Sall, had moved from Radford Woodhouse to Beeston Lodge. Ted told me many interesting things about Wollaton Park and I looked forward to meeting both gentlemen on the frequent visits I made there.

In the early eighties, someone happened to mention that Lionel had spent his childhood around Cherry Orchard and Radford Woodhouse. Needless to say, when next I saw him I broached him on this subject and as he began to recall his early life I remembered the pile of bricks in Shepherds Wood.

When I mentioned them Lionel nodded. Yes, they could only have been the remains of the two houses lived in by the Bakers and Wilsons. Both properties had fallen derelict over the years and the estate workers at Aspley Hall had raised them to the ground in the interests of public safety.

But Lionel still nurtures a good, long term memory and there are instances when one is listening to him that leave you with the distinct impression that his boyhood was the happiest time of his life.

RAMBLINGS AROUND NUTHALL AND BULWELL

Bordered by acres of fine parklands the village of Nuthall projected a deeply parochial atmosphere to such wanderers like my father who, when time permitted, enjoyed walking the lanes within a six or seven mile radius of his Nottingham home. Ayrshire and Dairy Shorthorn cattle grazed the fields alongside dray horses, shires and pit ponies, whereas the main crop yields were potatoes, turnips, barley and wheat.

St Patrick's church was always the hub of the community and its parishioners would boast of having retained a core of Nuthall characters. They were keen churchgoers and would talk about the skills of bellringing, the history of the famed Nuthall Temple, the trams and trolleybuses and the village notables, some of whom we shall be meeting in the following paragraphs.

On his walks from Bobbersmill to Nuthall, my father would encounter the occasional carrier's cart, a horse-drawn covered wagon, which conveyed mail, parcels, baggage and a few passengers from Nuthall to Nottingham with both pub refreshers and request stops in between.

One of the carter's first recognised stopping places was the Broxtowe Inn, where the drivers, and perhaps the passengers, partook in a pint or two of ale. From there, they proceeded to the Wheatsheaf at Bobbers Mill, where whiskey and gin could be obtained due to the pub having been granted a full licence.

At the beginning of the century, Nuthall's main street was little more than a rough track along which a horse-drawn water cart would sprinkle the shale surface to settle the dust during spells of warm weather. By contrast, rain soon reduced this track to a width of mud and sludge, which clung to the shoes and boots of passers by and caused youths to skid when they were riding their brakeless 'boneshaker' bicycles over the uneven surface. Many of these early contraptions had been fitted with wooden wheels, and the youths lost no time in

challenging one another to high speed rides down the hill from Kimberley and
into Nuthall village.

Timber hauliers with load secured for transportation to the sawmills.

My father could just about recall the gas lamps in the churchyard being pulled
down on a chain, so that the tapers were lit and the parishioners guided directly
to the church porch, as they wended their way to a service in the early winter
darkness. But whenever he told someone that he had just walked back from
Nuthall, my father was always asked if he had seen the unique manor house
known as Nuthall Temple.

Built by Sir Charles Sedley, the local Squire, in 1747 the so-called temple
was designed to represent an Italian villa, with all the fixtures and fittings
expected of a building bearing such eminence. There were stone staircases, a
double perra and balustrade, tapestries, carpets and many ornate drapes and
ornaments. It was also equipped with art galleries, libraries, and a billiard and
music room. The Sedleys bred racehorses which were trained so efficiently that
several became winners of world renown and helped swell the family fortunes.

Over the years the Temple became the inheritance of the Reverend Robert Holden who was the son of the local Squire. After serving as Rector for over thirty years, he became the Squire himself in 1913 and the researcher should not confuse this gentleman with the several Robert Holdens who had preceded him. Engrossed with the parish and its history he wrote a book called 'An Ancient Yew Tree's Story', compiled a Nuthall Temple Inventory and finalised a scrap-book of notes and observations which was eventually donated to the County Records Office.

It was during his time that the spelling of the village's singular name of Nuthall was gradually transformed into Nuttall. But the Reverend Robert Holden objected, and after two or three attempts, was able to persuade the parish council that he merely intended to right a wrong and not perpetrate an error any further'.

Thus his beloved village became known as Nuthall and the school headmaster Mr George Gleadlow informed his pupils by correcting their exercise books in red ink each time the word Nuthall appeared. The postmaster had also to adjust to the new spelling, though he had been among those who opposed the change but eventually noted that the Squire had managed to get his way.

Robert Holden was also remembered for his scholarly looks and the fact that he wore a white tie instead of the traditional white collar of the cleric. After Robert Holden's death the Temple fell into a state of disrepair but not before the auctioneers moved in and sold the fixtures and fittings in 1929.

The sum of fifty pounds was paid for the entrance staircase along with two stone sphinxes. These and additional fittings were transported to Cromer, Norfolk by rail and were included in the ornamental design of a house near that resort. Soon after the sale it was decided that the Temple's remaining structure was unsafe after having stood for only 175 years.

Presumably the parish council called in a team of local contractors who soaked the wooden props in paraffin then set fire to them. Eventually the fire demolished each section of the fine house and, as one can imagine, besides the glare and roar from the flames the clouds of smoke and dust had the enthusiasts moving back and winding handkerchiefs over their mouths. The M1 motorway passes over the exact site of the Temple today but the still lovely lake partially surrounded by trees, lends a serene atmosphere to the periphery tracts of land some of which is water meadow bordered by regenerated sycamore woodland while, beyond the trees, fine rambling acres have been included as part of the grounds and gardens surrounding well hidden houses of individual character.

My father never mentioned having seen the lake for when he was a boy it was enclosed within the Temple grounds. But had he been caught there by a gamekeeper or local policeman, or 'bobby', he may well have had his ears clipped for having wandered where he shouldn't.

If he missed the lake however, he made up for it eventually by riding on the trams. Once the residents of Kimberley heard that the tram routes had been laid they flocked to embark on the journey through Nuthall and Bobbersmill and alighted in Nottingham where some spent the entire day or evening. People lined the aisles and stairs when all the seats were taken. When two trams met on a single track one had to back until the driver reached a terminal point and, apparently, this caused disruption among the passengers who encouraged the drivers to argue about which had the right to progress according the time and location along a particular route.

Thus as we can imagine, there were boos and jeers although two trams meeting headlong on the track wasn't an everyday occurrence by any stretch of the imagination. The horse-drawn trams that my grandparents and great grandparents had known were soon given the localised name of 'plodders' and the trip from Basford, Nuthall or Bulwell, took so long that some considered the carriers carts to have been a more satisfactory mode of transport, though perhaps with good reason, considering that they stopped alongside at least two public houses along the route!

But the day was not so far distant, when the route planners employed by the Nottinghamshire and Derbyshire Tramway Company decided to lay a track along the fifteen-mile route from Ripley to Nottingham. They also included passing points to avoid those ugly arguments arising. One of these was constructed in the centre of Nuthall village.

Although the railway companies were providing adequate services to the outlying villages and hamlets the trams proved a much cheaper means of travel particularly since stopping points were placed wherever there was a row of farm cottages or colliery community.

The new trams were double-decked with wooden seats. The first fleet consisted of twenty-four. The first livery was light green lined with gold but, in later years, the green shade became brighter and the gold occasionally replaced by a bordering of cream. Half the fleet was covered by a roof; the other half remained open to the elements thus on a rainy day everyone crowded onto the lower deck.

So mechanisation came to Nuthall and the surrounding areas. Standards were erected, wires laid, trees were felled or the branches lopped. Some old buildings were also demolished so that the track could be widened and eventually D.H. Lawrence perceived tramcars 'plunging into the industrial countryside, tilting away in a rush past cinemas and shops, making reckless swoops downhill and waiting in the hilltop market place before the breathless slither down the drop'.

The 'hilltop market place' he mentioned would have been Heanor. The first Nuthall section of tramlines were completed in March 1913 although a few further adjustments needed to be made. The first tram journey was made in the August of that year, the pilot route being from the tram depot at Langley Mill to Cinderhill.

The following year the trams began running from Ripley to Nottingham stopping at Heanor, Eastwood, Kimberley, Nuthall, Basford, Bobbersmill and any request points between. The journey took almost three hours! Besides the driver there was a conductor who carried a whistle and ensured that sections of the track were kept clear of children, dogs and wandering cattle. Even in those days the passengers grumbled about paying the fare and many people were wary of the lines which, they conceded, could produce a severe electric shock. So along with films of Buster Keaton, Tom Mix and Laurel and Hardy my father and his generation, became well acquainted with the local trams and one or two of the people connected with them.

Nuthall, drew my father, like a magnet and in pubs such as The Stag at Kimberley or the Horse and Groom near Moorgreen he learned about the local characters and men who were well respected due to their services to the community. Some of the men he met spoke of Mr Gleadow who was the Nuthall schoolmaster with a reputation for severity in the classroom. Being the organist and choirmaster at St Patrick's church he recruited boys for the choir, gave magic lantern shows and organised midsummer charabanc outings to places of local interest such as Wollaton Hall or Newstead Abbey. His wife was the school's sewing mistress for a time and when, after retiring, her husband died in 1927 she still attended the church services but lived for only another five years. In those days a boy was liable to be caned for throwing up at a tree, repeatedly climbing a fence or telling a lie. Yet most schoolmasters were sympathetic toward the land and its harvest and little was said if a boy had a few days off to help with the potato pickings or assisted with setting them in rows across the fields.

One man whom my father would liked to have met left school to become a shoemaker then filled his stepfather's position of parish clerk. His name was Shadrack Starr. Shadrack's life revolved around all the church activities. He was responsible for maintaining the parish records, helping at all the services and such varied occasions as weddings, baptisms and funerals. He was also a scholar in that he could read and write and sing quite well.

Besides his parish duties, Shadrack ran the Nuthall post office from his house on Main Street. The House, I should add, stood alongside the formal entrance lodge to Nuthall Temple. Shadrack was the type of man described by many as 'the last of his kind'. This was particularly true in the occupational sense because after he died the post of parish clerk was never filled, and vergers and sextons were appointed to share 'the tasks among themselves. Wearing a three-quarter length black coat and a flat hat with a wide brim, Shadrack Starr was described as a distinguished looking man, honest to the last word and keen to read at the lectern. But by the time my father had begun to acquaint himself with the village, the old parish clerk had quietly passed away at the age of eighty-seven. He was to be remembered for many years and people spoke his name in the same semi-hushed tones as Mr Gleadow, for as long as the old village was able to retain its Victorian/Edwardian image.

A man who was still wandering the fields and woods when my father was a young man wore a battered trilby beneath which tresses of silvery white hair cascaded down to his collar. He clutched a stick with one hand and usually had a sizeable basket strapped over his back and shoulders. Wearing a belted raincoat that had seen better days, the man walked with a sack tied protectively across his shoulders during times of hard or inclement weather and sacking was also wound around his trouser legs. When he wasn't roaming the woods and fields, helping the sexton at St Patrick's church or attending a service either at Christmas, Easter or the Harvest Festival, this gentleman sought out mushrooms and berries or collected kindling before retiring to his lodgings in a nearby farmhouse.

From casual conversations struck up, in the public houses my father learned that this wanderer was known as Old Jim Cargill. Locally popular due to his wisdom and funds of stories gained when he was employed as a farmworker, and had served as an officer in the Yeomanry, Jim Cargill was also the landlord of a Kimberley hostelry before he chose to lead the free life which terminated with his sudden death on Christmas Eve 1927.

I remember my father shaking his head and saying 'Fancy dying on Christmas Eve, eh?', after he had related the passing of Old Jim to me. As a wide eyed boy, I wondered why Jesus hadn't bothered to postpone the poor man's demise – at least until the New Year.

After the last war I would sometimes be taken by my parents to the Three Ponds pub at Nuthall. These visits were usually made in the summer months and on a Sunday evening, with the threat of Monday morning lingering in my mind, as we sat on the low wall of the forecourt sipping our drinks.

Between nostril inflating sips of lemonade I would ask my parents if they had actually seen the ponds by which the public house had acquired its name. But there was always a negative reply and it wasn't until I had a young family of my own that I discovered there had indeed been three ponds draining down, I believe, into Temple Lake.

Although Nuthall has become a village ensnared within the urban fringe there is a roadside 'avenue of lime trees that interpret an awareness of both height and grandeur today as they have in times gone by. Whenever I travel that way, I am reminded of peaceful fields and, for a few moments, can forget the streams of traffic, the connecting hustle and bustle from the city to outlying housing estates. Suddenly I am plunged into an awareness of shire horses, haywains and red bricked farmhouses that can only be reached by walking a long dusty track which takes me over the crest of the hill to the nestling valley below.

There are few people with whom I can share this experience, although I feel that Shadrack Starr and Old Jim Cargill would have readily relayed the benefits of their parochial experiences had we met on some sequestered footpath in the long ago.

When they were courting in the early twenties, my parents often walked stretches of the River Leen. One of their favourite routes was across Bobbers-mill Fields and along the river bank to Basford where my father's sister, Aimey, ran the sweet shop in Lincoln Street.

Whether they walked to Bulwell town or caught a tram or bus I cannot be sure. But both my parents knew the stretches of the Leen between Bulwell and Moorbridge at Bestwood extremely well and when recently I met an elderly man, leaning on the balustrade, he endorsed, almost word for word, my parents' descriptions of the river as they had known it throughout the twenties and thirties. The man had spent his boyhood at nearby Moorbridge Cottages, close to the river, the mineral railway line and two or three marshy pools.

"Aye it hasn't changed all that much since I was a lad. On hot summer days we used to dive in from the railway bridge", said the man gesturing toward the buttresses that supported the railway lines.

"There were trains coming along and men working on the line but we didn't bother. Often we swam naked; diving straight in among the frogs and the fish. And when we weren't swimming we were netting the river and pulling out roach, sticklebacks and crested newts."

Turning then to face Bulwell he pointed downstream and continued:

"There were some lovely millpools situated behind the factories and dye-works on the main Bulwell – Hucknall road. In summer these pools were partially obscured by bulrushes and thickets of willow or osier. We'd see moorhens and mallard with their ducklings and every other millpond had a pair of swans nesting in the bulrushes.

"There were butterflies too! Any amount of 'em and, being lads, we swam and waded wherever and whenever we could although our parents always told us to keep away from the huge mill-wheels because a lad, who was once swimming beneath one as a dare, had a limb severed straight from his body.

In the severe winters that we used to have then it was a completely different world. In fact, you'd hardly have recognised it from the one we knew in summer. All the millpools iced over like thick sheets of glass and almost everyone who could afford ice skates came down at the weekends.

On Saturday and Sunday afternoons you'd see young couples, clutching one another and gliding along while they laughed and joked or murmured endearments. But we lads were there with the intention of trying to knock lads of around our own age onto the ice. When there was a real hard freeze up and everywhere was covered with snow men would appear as if from nowhere and set up little stalls along the river bank from which they'd sell hot potatoes and potatoes roasted in their jackets. When they put these in a paper parcel for you there was an added dimension to be gained because you were aware that they'd just been lifted from the red hot embers of a brazier.

Yes. I can see us all there now. Clutching our ice skates and munching hot potatoes, dressed as we were in top coats and with woollen scarves wound around our necks. And do yer know, it doesn't seem five minutes ago really."

Some of Bulwell's residents used to collect watercress, packed into little wicker baskets and sell it at the weekend market held in the centre of the town. The best cress beds were to be found at Moorbridge and George Bramley, whose recollections feature in the next chapter, lived at Moorbridge Cottages with his wife and young family some thirty or forty years ago.

"It was lovely in the summer. Some seasons you'd look out of the front window and see a swan sitting a clutch of eggs among the reeds of one of the marshy pools. When the cygnets hatched they'd just lead them over the derelict field to the river and here they would spend the rest of the year.

In the autumn and winter though the cob would chase off his cygnets and I used to watch them surging across the water like white galleons and the brown and white youngsters skitting across the surface in front of them. Farther along Moor Road Bestwood was a backwater alongside which refuse was dumped by the authority represented today by the Ashfield Council. Another pair of mute swans capitalised on the reed beds here and also hatched off a cygnet brood."

Swans and cygnets, much as George Bramley would have seen them on the lake at Springhead

George would similarly watch this pair chasing off their young. Like the man I met at Moorbridge George was made very much aware of such fish as the stickleback, roach, tench and perch. Warm spring evenings also ensured that if they slept with their bedroom windows open, the residents of Moorbridge Cottages would be serenaded throughout the night by the consistent croak of countless frogs.

A damp and foggy place in winter, Moorbridge proved itself to have been a countryman's haven in the spring and summer. ''We were surrounded by wildlife,'' said George, ''and no matter where you live – you can't do better than that.''

YESTERDAY'S FIELDS – FARMSTEADS AND FAMILIES

The aptly-named 'Royal Hunt' is a relatively new public house situated just off the main Nottingham Hucknall road. Beyond it the rooftops of two, widely spread housing estates, Rise Park and Top Valley, hide the hills and ridges that sweep like a shelving staircase toward the woods of what is now the Bestwood Country Park.

It was at the Royal Hunt that I had arranged to meet George Bramley and Frank Hopkin for a lunchtime pint, and hopefully make some notes as they reminisced about their early days spent roaming the woods and fields on which many of West Nottingham's housing estates now stand.

Both George and Frank are in their eighties yet look twenty years younger. As we shook hands I noticed George's shock of soft white hair and Frank's straight back as he sat at the table with his pipe curving downward from his lips and pint glass placed on the polished table top before him.

The two men used to meet here every Thursday but their friendship goes back well beyond retiring age for as boys George and Frank attended the same school and, when it was possible, sat next to one another in the classroom.

After we had settled I began by asking George if he could possibly recall something of his formative years and in no time discovered that despite his years he has a remarkable retentive memory.

His story really begins with the meeting of the two young people who were to become his mother and father for both were employed at Springhead House situated behind the Babbington Colliery and with its formal entrance and drive leading out onto Cinderhill Road.

Springhead House was originally built for the Charles family who were the local dyers and finishers. The house was built in our great grandfather's time and most of the district's able young men were employed there as builders. One such youngster was another George who carved his name on the rail bannister before the new owners had moved in and was subsequently sacked for his misdemeanour.

Springhead House near Bulwell. Once the home of Dr Neilson, and where George Bramley's parents met.

George Bramley's father was employed as a gardener at Springhead House and his mother was nursery maid to the two sons of Doctor Neilson and his wife who acquired the property when the Charles family moved elsewhere. Before she married George's mother accompanied the Neilsons and their sons on what was to be the trip of a lifetime, for one summer the family chartered a luxury cruiser and toured the Western Isles of Scotland.

When they returned Dr Neilson combined his practise alongside that of another local medic Dr Candlish and occasionally the latter gentleman, and his wife, visited his partner at the splendid house for a lawn party or just to stroll the grounds.

I have already mentioned the fact that the house and grounds faced Cinderhill Road. On entering the formal gateway ones gaze rested upon the artificial lake on the left then the path led slightly uphill to higher ground from where a spring tumbled down from a higher pool which held a great many goldfish. At the head of this pool was a rockery and grotto from which natural spring water appeared and fed the small and larger stretches of water accordingly.

The house was fronted by a lawn and rose gardens. After his parents married and settled down in a terraced house in Bradford Street George was born and not surprisingly, Springhead House and its grounds became his second home.

He remembers two cars parked outside the house; one a fine Austin A55, the other an early Ford, probably a Model 2. The Neilson's chauffeur was called Frank Noble. The young couple continued to work for the Neilsons when their two sons and two daughters were still quite small and another of George's earliest recollections was that of snuggling into his mother's lap in a rowing boat with his father working at the oars and his mother throwing small portions of their picnic over the side and attracting a pair of mute swans and their cygnets over to feed.

George said reflectively: "The swans used to nest on the island of the lake at Springhead then when the cygnets were growing and needing more aquatic food than the lake could nurture they would leave the lake and walk in line down the gravel drive with the cob leading then cross Cinderhill Road, filed down the street opposite then go down the steep bank to the River Leen's marshes, or 'willow woods' as we eventually came to call them. And here they spent the rest of the year. Can you imagine two swans and a line of little cygnets trying to cross Cinderhill Road today?" George asked, and both Frank and I had to admit that we couldn't.

In my mind's eye, at least, were blocks of prefabs bordered by dusty privet hedges, a valve depot and crocodiles of bumper to bumper traffic passing from daybreak to dusk.

Another memory that George carries of his boat trips on the lake, features the doctor's wife Mrs Neilson who used to sit in the boat opposite the boy when he was older and read him stories from a book entitled 'Tanglewood Tales' by Nathaniel Hawthorn.

She would always begin by asking: "And with what story shall we begin today then George?" But my friend had his favourites among them and just as the good lady asked the same question each time she had the book in her lap so her pupil chose the same story to begin with.

"It was almost a foregone conclusion that she would ask the question and I would name the same story. But I never tired of hearing it and if I'd said anything different I think she'd have fallen back into the lake with surprise," chuckled my friend.

When the Neilsons left Springhead House, another family moved in but eventually it was taken over and used as offices by the National Coal Board. The surrounding parklands were divided up into allotments and the lake allowed to revert to its natural state. George can still remember the fine mature trees in the grounds and when he was in the passenger seat of a car some time ago he also recognised the stone pillars that had supported the wrought iron gates of Springhead House. Ironically these pillars and another set of gates now stand aloof in the middle of the small prefab estate. The lake was never recognised as such by the allotment holders of the 1950s for most of them referred to it as floodwater. In the early sixties it was finally drained, but to what purpose is difficult to determine.

Throughout his boyhood and youth George lived with his parents and brothers and sisters at the house in Bradford Street but beyond the busy streets of Bulwell the higher country beckoned; the wild scrublands, deep sided valleys and green sloping meadows grazed by herds of cattle; and I discovered that George and Frank were eager to talk about the fields of Bestwood over which they had wandered in their younger days. Pointing back over his shoulder with the stem of his pipe George asked if I had seen the strip of old railway line running parallel to Hucknall Road then explained that this had been a local mineral line which passed between the ancient banking known as Bestwood Deerleap.

In medieval times, such leaps were constructed purposely to introduce fresh blood into the deerpark and Bestwood Park had several leaps constructed around its boundaries. A deer-leap was designed to enable the wild forest deer to leap down to join the stock in the deerpark but they were unable to return to their more familiar grazings because the walls and bankings upon which each leap was set were higher than the animals could leap to get back.

Deer had been harboured at Bestwood since time immemorial and both James I and Richard III hunted there. But such accounts belong to much earlier years yet thankfully past historians have researched into, and mapped out, the ancient boundaries and that strip of mineral line is still known as Bestwood Deer-leap to this day.

The line of oaks flanking Hucknall Road and the mineral line was planted as a boundary marker for the Bestwood deerpark which was eventually called the St Albans estate. Turned over to farming land some two or three hundred years ago, the land was described by Rider Haggard in 1902 as being 'sandy and given up to the production of sheep, turnips and barley; the grasslands being poor'. George believes that Haggard was referring to the tract of land that divides Southglade Road and Arnold Road.

Trees and hedgerows are today seldom recognised as having been intentionally planted as field boundaries. The dominant trees here are Black Poplars

"This was scrubland. Hawthorn thickets growing on a ridge of sand. A real wilderness where willow warblers nested and sang throughout the summer and rabbits were about all the year round."

But cattle were grazed heavily on all the main pastures when George and Frank were boys and both agreed that: 'there were any number of pheasants, partridges and hares about'. Badgers were also well dug in. Both in the fields and hedgebanks and across in Big Wood, on the other side of the ridge. There were three or four setts, but nobody ever bothered them then like they do today; not even the farmers or gamekeepers.

Local people gathered berries to make wine and the fields in early summer were pebble-dashed with cowslips. The farms in the immediate vicinity had been given attractive names with Sunrise Hill Farm perhaps being the foremost among them.

George and Frank however spent most of their free time at Southglade Farm with Farmer Jarvis Goddard, as he liked to be known. They recalled summer days spent hay-making. The shire horses pulling hay-carts. The local game-keeper shooting woodpigeons, hares and rabbits. Autumn mornings spent collecting mushrooms and bluebuttons. Summerclad girls coming home from the woods cradling masses of bluebells between their bare arms.

Every fine Sunday morning Farmer Jarvis Goddard and a companion rode around the Bestwood field boundaries. Occasionally they called on the neighbouring farmers probably to discuss cattle market prices, farming machinery or look over a new bull or stallion bought for the stud. Within a mile or so of Southglade Farm and Top Valley Farm stood Low Valley Farm so called because a sand track led between two hills with the farm nestling in the valley below.

From his seat in the lounge bar of the Royal Hunt, George pointed beyond a window and said, "See that single oak tree there. Well the track to Low Valley Farm went by the left side of it, then you walked under a little railway tunnel which was just wide enough for the farmer to get his tractor through.

The conversation changed then to include a visit to the Basford Miners' Welfare and I asked my friends if they knew how the lake in the grounds had become known as Fowlers Pond; a venue to which we boys of the Ellis Secondary School walked and explored two or three times a year.

"It was probably the Fowlers family who had lived at Basford Hall before it was taken over by the Welfare Committee" George explained while I explored the possibility of the lake being a favourite location for the local wildfowlers and named accordingly.

Fowlers Pond had apparently been fed by a very pretty stream which meandered from the equally lovely lake in the grounds of Nuthall Temple. "I think it was called Nuthalls Stream", said George then mentioned rambling around the nearby Hempshill Farm and passing though a kissing gate to Hempshill Hall. This residence was built on the site of a medieval chapel. It first was tenanted soon after it was built around fifteen-sixty. Today, I should add, Hempshill Hall is still a private residence and closed to the public or curious historian.

On a slope below the Hall a derelict cottage surrounded by trees always attracted young boys particularly since it had the reputation for being haunted. George's birthplace of 'Springhead' was to be found just to the west of this site, and as he recalled the lake a second time I was prompted to ask him about the exact whereabouts of Farrands Dam. The name of this mill dam came as something of an environmental shock to me when I was about seven years old and walking with my father along Valley Road which is part of the Nottingham ring road.

As we were passing a block of council houses, beyond Barlock Road, my father stopped beside an oak tree rising from a council house garden and said: "When I was a young man you turned along a little track here that wound across the fields to Farrands Dam".

Mystified, I stared at the houses for it had never occurred to me that houses and factories had been built on tracts of countryside that now only existed within the minds of those old enough to remember them. "Farrands Dam! What was it like Dad? Where is it today", I chimed. "Gone. Built on. Beneath all these houses and gardens", my father replied. When we were back home at Chalfont Drive he drew me a rough map of how the dam was shaped and on its western bank filled in a large square that depicted the mill.

"There were reeds growing alongside the mill and every year a pair of swans used to nest there and rear a brood of cygnets", he continued.

George Bramley believes the dam was fed by the little Daybrook, which was a relatively fast flowing stream diverting the water from the drainage ditches and high fields of Arnold, Bestwood and Mapperley.

The mill dam had probably originated from natural swampland caused by the Daybrooks winter floodings. He went on to explain that, in the twenties, Farrands Dam was owned by the Greenhelge family who ran a cotton doublers business. This, then prompted me to ask the obvious question – "What on earth was a cotton doubler". "Well doubling involved the task and motions of winding the cotton from the cup to the cone," my friend explained. "Farrands Dam? It was a beautiful stretch of water. Very reedy. With swans and some lovely extensive beds of white water lilies, in the season," he continued.

Throughout the autumns of his boyhood George and his companions went on 'nutting parties'. Carrying jars and canisters they harvested the hedgerows for hazel nuts and the groves for sweet chestnuts. Big Wood which trails down from the highest point of Bestwood to the colliery village was, then, still closely patrolled by gamekeepers who chased the local nutting parties in no uncertain manner. But eventually the boys heard of the vast crops of hazel and sweet chestnuts that were to be found at Aspley. Packing up their dinners they set out on a Saturday or Sunday for what might then have been called 'The Bakers Territory'; Aspley Hall, Shepherds Wood, Horseshoe Wood, Robins Wood, Cherry Orchard and Radford Woodhouse.

"Each time we came back across the hills and vales of Broxtowe, Cinderhill and Bulwell laden with jars of blackberries and raspberries and satchels filled with hazels and sweet chestnuts. Sometimes after a scuffle or two with 'the Cherry Orchard youths' George added while smiling quietly to himself at the same time.

Nuthall, which was much closer to Bulwell and Bestwood, is thought to have been so named by the Anglo Saxons because of its reputation for producing rich, autumnal harvests of hazel nuts.

"But they were never so big, nor tasted quite the same as those from Aspley and Cherry Orchard; at least not when we were lads," George confirmed.

When the First World War broke out, George's father was called up for service and when he was eventually demobbed found work as a quarryman. But unfortunately he died about six weeks before his fiftieth birthday and then the old Bradford Street house began to see several changes, one of which revolved around George's brother who emigrated to Australia.

When George married a local girl he moved with his young bride to a house close to the River Leen and its marshes at Moorbridge, Bulwell. Bulwell is thought to have acquired its name simply because one of the several pools close to Moorbridge were used by the herdsmen who followed Bulla, a Saxon chieftain. Thus the pools became collectively known as Bulla's Well the place where his cattle slaked their thirsts. Local folklore on the other hand dismisses Bulla completely and lays emphasis upon the stature of a great bull which in a fit of fury plunged his horns deeply into the rocks and when he withdrew them attempted to drink the clear water that suddenly spurted from a fissure in which lay a deeper source.

The house in which George lived is standing to this day; a two-storey building at the rear and three-storey at the front, facing Moor Road which leads to Bestwood Village. Instead of going downstairs to the cellar you went upstairs, from the kitchen, and although it was an austere place in the winter, with the mist creeping in across the reeds it was a haven throughout the spring and summer when willow and reed warblers were singing and legions of frogs were chorusing on warm nights while George and his wife slept with the windows opened wide.

When the Second World War broke out, George was not called for service because he was employed at Rolls Royce, Hucknall and his work therefore was considered to have been the equivalent of being recruited into the ranks and serving on the defensive front line.

When George's sons and daughters came along he lost no time in making them aware of the changing seasons and the small but thriving wilderness spread around the house. "Then as the children got older they also became acute observers and we used to watch the kingfishers hunting for minnows between Moorbridge and the Forge Mills. We'd see water voles too. And it was at Forge Mills that I once spotted a lovely white barn owl hovering in the dusk.

When I went home I told my wife and the next night I took the children up to see it. There was a bus terminus on the main Bulwell – Hucknall road then just as there is today and the owl got the habit of perching on a post then, when the bus turned around, he'd go swooping towards it perhaps with the intention of catching any insects or cockchafers caught up in the jetstream.

By the way – although a few people called it Moorbridge, in those days we locals always knew it as Gambolls Bridge and it was a hump-backed structure spanning the width of the Leen; not a bit like the one that's there today.

Some winters, as we have seen elsewhere, the river froze from bank to bank and beyond the dank, misted marshes the fields of Southglade and Top Valley took on a decidedly austere atmosphere especially during the heavy snowfalls. People went sledging then on the slopes but I think most of the farming families must have realised that they were cut off by snowdrifts in the same way as the farmers of Exmoor and Dartmoor.

George smiled again as he began to recall the long winter evenings. Back thumbing over his shoulder again he said, "That railway line we mentioned. The one that crosses the deer-leap embankment and runs beside the boundary oaks. Well, along there was Wrigleys' Railway Wagon Works. The family came into business after one of their number invented the patent for the grease box that was used for greasing the axles of the railway trucks."

He then went on to explain that the family set up a social club for its employees. This was housed in a long wooden hut where men drank and played darts, dominoes and brag until the small hours of the morning.

But not only was the club popular with the Wrigleys' employees, for it was visited regularly by the constable on the beat, who was aware that drinking and gambling continued long after hours, but overlooked these misdemeanours just as long as he was served his free pint of ale. If this constable learned that a group of higher ranking police officers were scheduled to tour the district at around club closing time he would telephone the social club from an outside call-box and the steward would ensure that he closed the doors on time and everyone left at the appointed hour.

One freezing night, however, there was a sudden and authoritative knock on the door which interrupted all the social activities. After withdrawing the bolt and lifting the latch the club steward found himself confronted by a police sergeant and a constable who hustled in and to everyone's relief said: "Carry on lads. We've come to join you!". On another occasion a police superintendent and four detectives, joined the throng. Other 'outside' regulars included the local farmers and farmworkers.

The farmer from Sunrise Hill Farm, whose name George has forgotten, used to take cardboard boxes tightly packed with new laid eggs down to the club. He gave one egg to every man present the intention being that he should put it into his beer and it was not long before Sunrise Hill's beer and egg evenings became a regular event at the Wrigley's Social Club, as did the evenings that Farmer Jarvis Goddard strolled in carrying a wicker basket filled with potatoes baked in their jackets and packed with straw so that some of the warmth was retained after he had left the farmhouse and walked down through the night-blackened fields to the welcoming light in the valley below.

Today George Bramley lives opposite the Southglade School complex in the house that he has occupied for the last forty-one years. George I should add is eighty years old (June 1990). Goddards Farm stood nearly opposite the school's main entrance he told me, and after he sold the land to the Nottingham City Council, Farmer Jarvis Goddard became a patrolman on the few remaining acres of his former land that was designated for people's enjoyment; the Southglade Sports Centre and Playing Fields complex. He died in 1989.

Pointing over the railings separating the schools complex from the pavement George further told me that there had once been a lovely valley there, well thicketed but little more than twenty-five feet deep.

While riding around the estate on a local bus, he pointed again to the hedge row bordering the road known as the Ridgeway. "This hedge, and the others that lead off from it, are about all that's left of the old Bestwood fields. The hedges, these few fine old trees, the dips and swerves in the landscape, and me."

While George and I had been engaged in conversation, Frank had been given ample time to recall his own experiences especially those gleaned when he was employed as a delivery boy by Woolleys, a Bulwell-based firm of bakers and confectioners.

"Why I rubbed shoulders with the gentry and knocked on the doors of country houses that aren't even standing today. It's incredible what can happen to a landscape in the space of seventy or eighty years."

Each morning Frank and his mate rigged up a pony and trap at the confectioners then spent their day delivering bread, cakes and pastries to all the manor houses and farms in the neighbourhood. Despite hoar frost, blizzards and fog they were expected to call on each customer twice a week.

Their day began by harnessing the pony to the trap in the confectioner's stableyard at the rear of their premises. Once in the seat of the trap they sent the trot pony along Cinderhill Road then guided it up long, hilly Bells Lane around by the Broxtowe Hall Estate to Strelley Village which is recognised as the highest point in Nottingham. The last farm on the left before the road swings abruptly right and by-passes Strelley church, was managed by the Wellburn family. It was here in the field alongside the Wellburn's dutch barn that the confectioner's second pony was kept.

Here, the two lads would harness the pony and let it into the field then by feeding sugar lumps or oats to the second pony they were able to back it into

the shafts of the cart and harness it in readiness for the round trip ahead. A
routine of this nature ensured, of course, that one pony was rested one day while
the other was put to work. Thinking back to the trip between Bulwell and
Strelley Frank said

"Bells Lane in those days was just wide enough for two farmcarts or horse
drawn dreys to pass. Bells were probably a family who once tenanted a farm
owned by the residents of nearby Broxtowe Hall. Nobody's fully certain how
the name was linked with that long ridge but you can bet it didn't derive purely
from a casual or accidental source. From the seat in the pony cart you saw fields
that were ploughed by a two-horse team in the autumn become rich with golden
corn by the end of the summer. Herds of Ayrshire and Dairy Shorthorn cattle
grazed the lusher fields.

On the west side of the lane, almost screened by trees, stood Broxtowe Hall
which was owned by the Bramley family – who were local timber merchants
and, unfortunately, not related to my lifelong friend George so far as we are
aware.

The local gossips used to tell us that there was always a little bit of rivalry
taking place between Squire Edge of Strelley Hall and the Bramleys of
Broxtowe. Apparently the gamekeepers on these neighbouring estates were
constantly at odds with each other because one reckoned that the other
disregarded his employer's land boundary; and so it went on. Then the estate
owners themselves fell out over shooting rights, until a marriage was arranged
between the two families – and like your epic, best-selling novel – that settled
everything."

In the confectioner's pony and trap Frank and his mate made their twice
weekly deliveries to farms spreading from Strelley to Trowell, Kimberley,
Nuthall and Bulwell. After leaving the Wellburn's field at Strelley each
morning, they headed in a different direction according to the day of the week
but on two mornings called at The Strelley Broad Oak public house and the
gardener's cottage in which lived Mr and Mrs Dale who were employed by the
Edges of Strelley.

The gamekeeper's cottage was a traditional little red-bricked home in the
countryside set back off the main road, with a thick hedgerow screening the
garden and a paved path leading directly to the front door. Beyond it was the
parkland fence and two ponds where perhaps some earlier gamekeeper had
reared broods of mallard for the decoy and autumn shoots.

"I distinctly remember calling at The Strelley Broad Oak pub on my first
morning as a baker's delivery boy. After I had knocked politely on the front
door a voice beyond boomed: "Well come on in then! It's a bloody public

house'', and I opened the door tentatively to find myself confronted by an ill tempered little man whose voice you would hardly connect with someone of his build.

Once, when we were on a lane trotting between Strelley and Trowell, we turned a bend too sharply and keeled over into a snowdrift. Everything went over. The pony, trap, ourselves – the lot. But apart from all the smashed cakes and pastries there was no harm done but we rounded that bend with a little more care in the days and months that followed.

One really splendid house that we called at was Bulwell Wood Hall. But now there's nothing left of it save perhaps a photograph or two in the county archives office. It was built as the Dowager House to Newstead Abbey. After one of us rang the doorbell he'd be admitted by the butler who accompanied him up a magnificent oak staircase to the upper kitchen in which the head housemaid reigned supreme.

I always remember the framed portrait of a favourite racehorse displayed on the wall here because it had been hung to meet the eye when you turned left onto the landing.

The Broad Oak, Strelley, c.1919 (H Smith)

We also called at Bulwell Hall where we were usually met by the butler or head cook and then we guided the pony and trap along the lanes to Hempshill Vale Farm, Lyons Farm and Hootons Farm at Nuthall.''

But Frank's most vivid recollections revolved around the deliveries made to Redhill Lodge. The ornamental gates were once to be seen alongside the A609 road which connects Arnold to the Leapole roundabout.

"Today, you pass four estate cottages on the left side of the road as you're leaving Nottingham. There's a garage and stableblock there now if I'm not mistaken. Well the entrance to Redhill Lodge was situated somewhere around there.''

Redhill Lodge was owned at the time by Mr Harry Hardy who was a shareholder in the Hardy and Hansons brewery business, which was also known as Kimberley Ales. I was always fascinated by the shape and size of the Rolls Royce which was usually parked outside the Lodge and I never failed to have a second glance at the headlamps and the tyres which were painted white.

Mr Harry Hardy, as he was known, stood six feet four inches tall and was respected by every member of his household. If he happened to look out of the lodge window and saw us coming up the drive with the pony and trap he would shout his butler who would toss aside the 'Craven A' cigarette he had been smoking and come gushing and sweeping across the forecourt in his swallowtail coat shouting: "Yes Mr Harry. Coming Mr Harry. Right away Mr Harry''.

Now Mr Harry Hardy's gardener was a man called Webster and when Mr Harry required his services he'd stand at the door while he was paying his monthly account to us, look over our shoulders and bellow "Webster!'' – just like a company sergeant major. Needless to say, the gardener was there within seconds, hurrying towards his employer but exercising a little more personal restraint perhaps than the butler.

Webster, as I recall, always smoked a blend of tobacco called Ogden's Flake, and what particularly fascinated me was the tin which was corrugated on the underside so that you could strike a match across it. So there we were. A fine lodge house surrounded by pines and small paddocks with wrought iron fences. Ornamental gardens. A towering gentleman. Bowing and scraping butler. Slightly impatient gardener. Two delivery boys. A parked Rolls Royce; and a pony and trap.''

One bitterly cold day, the door of Redhill Lodge was opened by the housekeeper but Frank had received instructions from his employers to hand Mr Harry Hardy his account, personally.

"Well, if it's like that you had better go upstairs and see him then. He's in bed suffering from a very bad cold,'' she said.

Following the housekeeper's directions, Frank climbed the darkly shadowed, ornate staircase and timidly knocked on the bedroom door before he entered the room. Mr Harry was propped up on the pillows, pyjama clad and with a bottle of Johnnie Walker whiskey standing on the cabinet alongside his bed. A tray and whiskey glass had been placed close by.

After scrutinising the bill he thanked young Frank then said: "By the way son. It's still bloody cold out there, When you go down the stairs seek out my housekeeper and tell her to give you a good pint of my mulled ale to keep you warm".

After thanking the kindly man, Frank lost no time in doing exactly as he had been asked and at the same time wondered if Mr Harry would have recovered by the time he called again. Eventually, the pony and trap was replaced by a Morris Commercial van and the two lads travelled in comfort for a time.

When he was a little older Frank was employed by a firm of building contractors who specialised in repairing farm buildings. All the men engaged on each task were skilled at resettling pantiles after a night of strong gales, strengthening the roof structures of a Dutch barn and erecting conservatories and greenhouses. Consequently, they were never out of work. On his first morning young Frank reported to the foreman who gestured toward the parcel of sandwiches he was carrying

"Is that your lunch son?" the foreman asked.

When Frank told him that it was, the foreman said, "Well don't bother bringing any tomorrow because you'll be eating out. In fact you'll be eating out every day from now on".

By the next afternoon, Frank had worked out the foreman's ruse. After driving up to a farm, manor house or cottage they would take a rough estimate of the job that needed doing tben begin by working away from the house if this was possible. Towards noon however they would go to the house and look over the section that needed repairing. The foreman always made sure that the farmer's wife or lady of the house was around and able to speak with him. Usually he could steer a conversation around to the subject he wanted by asking if it would be all right to bring ladders or steps through the kitchen or leave them there while the repair gang had their dinner.

The farmer's wife would then say words to the effect of: "Oh yes. That'll be all right. And what are you having for your dinner?"

"Well we all usually bring a bit of bread and cheese" the foreman would answer.

"Bread and cheese! Is that all! That's no good for men who have seven or eight hours work to do! No. What you'd better all do is come into the house and have your dinner with us.'' Thus the matter would be settled and as the foreman had promised Frank dined out with amazing regularity throughout his years spent with the contracting gang.

Frank courted and eventually married a young lady who had once lived, three doors away from George Bramleys former home on Bradford Street. As a young husband he was eager to settle down in Bulwell and sought a steadier form of employment with regular hours. But he remembers the hustle and bustle of Bulwell, the corner shop tightly packed with almost every commodity a family could need, the mills, the dyeing and finishing works, Sankey's the plant pot manufacturers and the three large quarries that stood at the top of Commercial Road and were owned by the Jacksons, Clarkes and Culleys respectively.

He also remembers Bulwell Halt, a small railway station on the LNER line with a train especially laid on for the golfers visiting Bulwell golf course. However, this never became a paying proposition and that particular small local branch line was closed around 1934 due to lack of support. Both George and Frank are keen to point out that the so-called 'good old days' were good in some ways and not so good in others.

Expansion and over population has resulted in an obvious increase in the crime rate which both gentlemen find disturbing, while also mentioning the fact that sixty or seventy years ago everyone was so busily engaged in earning a living and helping those less fortunate than themselves, there was little time to think in terms of robbery with violence and civil wars seemingly nurtured by differences in religion.

"Why in our day you could go out and leave the doors of your house unlocked. You might be gone two or three hours; but everything would be just as you left it when you get back home,'' said Frank.

Nor have these two friends lost the warmth that was so obviously projected throughout the local communities in their younger days. On the contrary it has remained with them to the extent of each welcoming a stranger such as myself into their midst. And for that I am truly grateful.

A HERDSWOMAN'S RECOLLECTIONS

Mr and Mrs Walker, who are featured in this account, lived in two cottages built from local 'Bulwell' quarried stone. These single storey buildings were situated a few yards apart alongside a high hedge of hawthorn and blackthorn which provided shelter from the north easterly winds.

Having studied the map of Nuthall on Page 5 of the *Estate Publications Red Book of Nottingham*, I have noted the immediate location which is to be found in section D2 and would estimate the cottages to have been situated in the region of Seller's Wood Drive West, somewhere between Craster Drive and Hepple Drive.

It was in the mid-1970s that I came across the ruins of both buildings as I wandered the derelict fields with my eldest son. We had moved into a house on Langsdown Close and never able to resist the temptation to explore the surrounding countryside, we spent most summer evenings in the fields and woods watching fallow deer, foxes, kestrels and tawny owls.

We also stumbled upon the odd mound of housebricks or garden flowers extending across a small square or oblong of land, running parallel with the edge of a wood. Further investigations enabled us to discover some remnants of a boundary line or scraps of fencing and I concluded that a gamekeeper or woodman's cottage had once occupied the site.

The ruined cottages beside the hedge provoked my son into asking the questions I had asked my father when I was about his age. Who? When? Why here? It seemed almost as if I had never really left the derelict fields of the Cherry Orchard at Aspley for as I wandered beneath the two ivy-trunked elms, close to the ruins, I noticed some sizeable nettle beds extending along the hedgebank, found fragments of pottery and discovered the rusted frameworks of a double bed almost hidden by screens of dock leaves and hawthorn.

Still uncertain as to why the cottages had been built apart, and alongside a hedge perhaps over a hundred years ago, I walked along the hedgerow to the rib cage of a slewed aside farmgate and saw beyond it a green lane of velvet turf.

The stockman's cottage near Snape Wood, Bulwell, with artist Laura White's impression of how it may have looked at the turn of the century.

The track leading to Seller's Wood passed within yards of the ruins and I was reminded of the past each time that my son and I ventured out that way, although I had become resigned to the fact that I would never discover who had lived there. That same year, however I had occasion to visit a rest home for the elderly in the Blenheim district and, quite by chance, chose to sit beside a lady who had a round, pleasantly weathered face with long grey hair tied at the nape by a ribbon.

Her frequent smiles encouraged me to make conversation and I learned that she was suffering from arthritis but was feeling contented in her later years because she was among people and the knowledge that the streets of Bulwell were closer than before eased her mind considerably.

I asked if she had lived in a town environment before. She then mentioned Blenheim Lodge; a tall grey house in which my new acquaintance had been born. Her parents were herds-people or stockmen attached to the Blenheim Lodge estate. They did not live at the house but her mother was given a bed there during the time that she was in labour. A few weeks after the baby had been born the senior couple returned to the two cottages beside the hedgerow and the green ride. Mrs Walker spent a happy and carefree childhood there. When eventually she married, her parents moved into a house at Bulwell and the young couple took over their duties as stockman and herdswoman, as Mrs Walker was by then known.

The cottages were makeshift quarters really, she said. Rather than pay a local builder to build a cosy two-storey house for Mrs Walker's parents their employers apparently decided to get the job done as quickly and cheaply as possible and so, having known few types of houses other than those lived in by their friends and relatives, the young couple accepted this spartan accommodation that became the focal point in their lives.

Mrs Walker said: ''Yes. We lived in both cottages. We ate in one and walked alongside the hedge to sleep in the other. But in winter we ate and slept in the same one if we could manage it although it wasn't very pleasant with the smells of cooking still lingering in the air.

In winter, it was all mud. Mud, mud and more mud. Then when it snowed you were often ankle-deep in it, as you plodded to the stockpens to put hay and straw out for the cattle. Sometimes it was so cold that your fingers almost froze to the handles of the buckets you seemed to be forever carrying.

In winter, too, I'd skimp a bit on the washing and take it up to Blenheim Lodge if I could. I still had to do it myself though. But in summer my husband used to string a washline between those two elms in the hedgerow and I'd have my washing hanging out and stand outside the door with my dolly tub and ponch while fifty or sixty milking cows stood breathing down my neck. The cows were always standing around the front door watching you; just out of sheer curiosity.

People have said to me in the past 'I bet you were never bored'. But being a herdsman is anything but idyllic. All day long you're looking at cows. Twice a day you're staring at fifty or sixty backends and in those days we had to sit on a three-legged stool in the early morning and late afternoon and milk them turn by turn. It takes a lot of doing, milking by hand. So it was mainly hindquarters, udders, milk pails and cow slurry that we saw every day. There was very little time for anything else except cooking and washing your clothes.

We both used to herd the cows up to the farm first thing in the morning. After we'd milked about twelve cows each, my husband would start to pour the milk into bottles then put the bottles in crates while I carried on. Then, when all the milk was crated, we used to go across to the stable, feed the pony then harness it and back it into the shafts of the milk cart.

My husband used to eat an apple or something at about this time in the day, then he'd drive the milk cart out of the farmyard and start to make his deliveries in Bulwell, Basford and Nuthall while I herded the cows back into the fields.

If it was a nice day I'd do the washing next or put all the rugs and carpets on the line and beat the dust and dried mud out of them. This really used to bring the cows up to the cottage and they'd stand there watching me while I cussed the carpets and talked to each cow in turn.

Next I'd get the dinner ready and sometime between one and two my husband would come home. He was always cheerful but I've known the time when he'd be so tired he could hardly eat.

We'd have a quick nap after dinner, perhaps an hour just dozing in a chair. Then about half past three we'd wake, wash and take the herd back to the farm for another milking session.

I shopped in Bulwell about two mornings a week and we got fresh vegetables and eggs from the farm. Meat, we were able to buy cheaply because the farmer had an arrangement with the local butcher. In winter we had coal delivered by horse and dray but you couldn't have a very big fire in a cottage that size. But the day after a gale we'd try to make some time up so that we could go into the woods to collect kindling.

We'd often come home with arms filled with twigs and dragging a sack full of logs and branches that my husband had sawn in half. The gamekeeper kept us supplied with rabbits and at Christmas we were given the choice of a farmyard hen or a brace of pheasants.

Aye. In winter it was all mud and backache. Even now, as I'm sitting here, I can see in my minds eye two or three white enamel buckets that each held two gallons of milk or water. We'd often fill one of these up when we'd taken the cows into the stockyard for there was a tap situated along the wall beside the milking sheds.

We had to use the buckets first to swill the dung from the yard after we'd milked the cows then, when they were standing at the gate waiting to go back to the fields, either myself or my husband used to fill one or two buckets up again and carry them back to the cottage.

We used the same water from the same bucket for making tea, cooking, washing the dishes in and washing ourselves in. On bath night we'd settle into a galvanised bath in front of the fire like the colliers did. But on cold winter nights we weren't in the bath for very long, I can tell you that!

Oh yes, I hated the weight of those buckets tugging at my armpits and spilt water splashing down inside my wellington boots. You couldn't always hold the buckets away from your body even when you tried because you were wallowing in mud and cow slurry half the time.

We got to know all the cows and had names for each of them. Buttercup, Daisy, Stubborn, Deidre and so on. They knew exactly which stall to go in at milking time and you only had to hustle them if one or two of the herd leaders were slow in coming from the field.

When the farmer came round and decided which of them had to go for slaughter I always used to feel a bit sad. Then when the day came we either drove a little group into Bulwell, where a butcher's drover took over from us, or the slaughterman and several of his men would come up on a horse and dray.

We'd then drive a selected cow into a corner of the field and form a semi-circle round her till one of the men got close enough to put a rope around her neck. Then two or three of them would pull at the rope, shortening it all the time, so that the cow was brought down onto its knees.

To tell you the truth I never saw what used to happen after that because I always made sure I was walking back across the fields to the cottages but I do know that they were pole-axed and before the men lifted the dead, or dying, animal onto the dray they sometimes cut its throat so that the blood drained back into the earth and the job of cutting up the carcass would be easier in the abattoir.

But like everything, there were compensations and for me it was the time when the cows were calving. We'd put the heavily pregnant cows in a separate 'field and keep an eye on them. Some gave birth quite naturally. Others needed assistance and you'd find yourself following a cow that had got its offspring's head or hind feet protruding from its tail and couldn't go beyond that. So sometimes we'd rope the cow, guide her over to a corner of the field again and put our hands inside her if we couldn't get at the calf any other way. Then gently, but firmly, we'd work it out and you'd find that one might be trapped by a leg or have moved so that a great coil of umbilical cord had become wrapped around its body.

Oh, there were all kinds of situations. Occasionally you'd bring out a real big-boned bull calf and within hours it would have died. Simply because the effort was all too much for it. Other times you'd look at a frail little cow calf tottering about and think she was never going to make it and ten years later she'd be leading the next but one generation of cows into the milking shed. You just never knew what was going to happen when each parcel of jelly, sinew and umbilical cord was laying on the grass at your feet.

What I did love to see was the cow licking the calf all over just after it had been born. That way, the two animals get to know one another's scent. If a cow lost a calf and a calf was orphaned we used to put the two together if it was possible. But you could only achieve this by skinning the dead calf and fastening, or even sewing, its pelt onto the back of the living one. If you didn't do that the cow would usually reject it because the calf scent that she had got used to before her offspring died was different. So she wouldn't normally have allowed the orphan to feed on her milk. She might even have killed it out of the sheer frustration of wanting to keep it away from her udders. They can be that determined, can cows.

They talked too, you know. The cows lowing and their calves lowing back to them. We often used to dip our fingers in the milk pail and let the calves suck the milk off the end. You'd feel their rough little tongue caressing your finger tips. It was lovely. And they looked so innocent. Big dark oval eyes and oval heads. Rounded ears and rubbery noses. Oh, I could have filled both houses with them at times.

When you lived in one house during the winter, the other – the bedroom house, as it was meant to be – would get damp if you didn't attend to it regularly, so we'd collect kindling from the woods and light a fire in the small hearth there as often as we could. And that green lane you mentioned. It was just a mass of mud and hoofprints when we lived there. If it's velvety and looking good now it's because the cows of past years have trampled all over it and deposited their slurry back into the earth as fertiliser.''

When Mrs Walker paused to accept a cup of tea from one of the ladies who helped at the centre I asked her if she knew how Seller's Wood had got its name.

"Well I didn't know until recently. Although most woods are named after the man who planted them out or the woodsman who lived there. So I suspected that Seller's Wood had got its name from the same source and sure enough a group of people came walking up the bridle-road a few months before I left and we got talking about place names. One of them told me that Sellers was the woodsman who planted the original trees there in the seventeenth century.

I know that a lot of the trees are oak, but the thickets were mainly hazel and these historians also told me that Nuthall was named by the Anglo Saxons; because it was recognised as a good place for collecting nuts.

I must say that my husband and I used to harvest a lot. We'd collect basketfuls of hazel nuts and a few walnuts. Then we'd be out with our saucepans and a cauldron gathering blackberries, raspberries and elderberries for making wine. Goodness knows how we found the time! But we managed it somehow.

But while the winters were cruel the springs were idyllic. There were masses of wood anemones in the glades of Seller's Wood and then of course, the bluebells. And I know you're not supposed to pick wildflowers now but I did in the old days. I could never get enough vases. I'd get pots and vases filled with bluebells, and cowslips and pink and white campion out of the lanes.

Give or take the occasional whiff of cow manure, our little house in summer smelled of wildflowers and sunshine. In fact, I can smell the wild honeysuckle as I'm talking to you now."

Unfortunately, I have never seen Mrs Walker again although I have visited the centre. Another lady I met there described her as one who liked to be on her own and added that occasionally you'd see her staring into space and smiling quietly to herself.

I'd like to think that she was recalling those hard years she spent working as a herdswoman and the times when she paused to smell the sunshine and the wildflowers. Nor can the scent of wild honeysuckle be easily forgotten as Mrs Walker had begun to discover when she attended that centre for the elderly but at the same time chose to sit quietly and dream of those long forgotten fields that had served as both her workshop and her home.

SHAKING HANDS WITH D.H. LAWRENCE

As he walked towards me, commenting upon how badly the earth needed rain, I was immediately aware of John's presence for he stood square shouldered, straight backed and about five feet eleven inches tall.

Dressed neatly in an off-white jacket and dark brown trousers his manner of speech was easy; relaxed, and as we talked I estimated him to have been around sixty to seventy years old. But within minutes it became obvious that my estimate was way off the mark for he volunteered to mention that he was in fact ninety-one.

"Me? I was born in 1899, at Sutton in Ashfield. Although later the family moved to Eastwood. I can't remember a terrible lot about by mother because she seemed to be always surrounded by my sisters. It was almost as if they had formed a women's group of their own. But me and my brothers and our father, Jess, we had our own mens group; if you want to put it that way.

We were colliers. When I went down the pit, after I had left school-there was no machinery for extracting great blocks of coal like there is today. In fact, if you go to the Lound Hall Mining Museum near Retford you'll see an old sepia photograph of colliers hand-winding coal up to the surface. Well, one of those chaps could have been me because that's one of the jobs I used to have to undertake and the photograph was taken of Eastwood's colliers where I worked for some years.

As a young lad, going down in the cage with my dad, I never once lost that sense of creeping claustrophobia; until I was older that is. Nor did you ever really get used to the dark, even if you did have a lamp fitted into the top of your helmet.

It was intense, that darkness. Terrible. Almost mocking. Everywhere you looked there was blackness. We worked at the seams, kneeling almost as if we were destined to become victims of rheumatoid arthritis. Our backs were bent and we used to chew tobacco and chewing gum to keep our mouths moist. That way you didn't swallow so much rock dust.

So there we all were. Hour after hour. Day after day. Chiselling and chipping in near pitch-black darkness. We youngsters, we were told never to drink the ice cold water too fast because you'd get stomach cramps and chilled kidneys. So we learnt – a lot of us through bad experience – that luke-warm water was the best.

'Men Only' pub and skittle charabanc outing (Photograph: F.Parkes)

Yet I suppose in a way we were better off than the women and children who went down the mines years before. Oh, aye. There were women and children and they were employed to heave the wooden sledges on which the colliers stacked their coal lumps along the tunnels and passages.

My grandfather – or it might have been my great grandfather – I'm not certain – belonged to the generation of colliers who had to make their own wooden shovels and I think at Lound there's a collier's shoe on display that's estimated to have been down a mine for about three hundred years.

S'funny but I began believing more in God when I was working in the pits, and we always seemed to be going to church for christenings and marriages and the inevitable funeral.

And how we checked on those caged canaries that some men took down with them in the hope that the birds would sing if a cavern became infiltered with, what we called, killer gas. In a way we worshipped those little yellow birds because the gas could overtake a man before he knew what had hit him. But the birds of course warned us well in advance. By the fifties though, the Ringrose Firedamp alarm had been introduced and so we gradually dispensed with the canaries which were then kept at home, poor little things.

Then, of course, there were the pit ponies. Lovely little animals that hauled the sledges and small sturdy coal carts below ground. Some poor ponies spent their lives working underground and if they lived to an age when someone thought they should have been retired they were taken up and literally put out to grass. Mind you for about five minutes these retired ponies just stood looking at the grass and taking in lungfuls of comparatively pure air. They were disorientated beyond belief. And how we all spoiled them – both the retired ponies in the paddocks and those still hauling coal carts down the mine.

When he was down there each pony was fitted with a leather face mask. They were stabled and fed and never once ill treated I can assure anyone of that.

Yes, I lived and worked against a background of towering black headstocks and grey spoil heaps of slag and shale. Today, would you believe, the mine shafts are computerised. All streamlined and power controlled although the mines have still got names just as they had in my day although nowadays I think the best seams are the Parkgate, Blackshale, Deep Soft and Deep Hard. at least, so I've heard it said.

Life above ground, such as it was, well that was bonus time to most of Nottinghamshire's colliers. Usually they took a keen interest in football, gambling, pitching the horseshoe, fishing and flying racing pigeons.

If you were a racing pigeon enthusiast then you had a loft installed in the yard of the small back-to-back terraced house in which you lived. And when you got your bicycle out of the shed on Sunday morning, put a wicker basket filled with pigeons on your pannier and cycled out to some high point where you released them, then the awareness of freedom you experienced was unbelievable.

Racing pigeons were an emblem of freedom to a collier. He sat on his hillock taking in great lungfuls of air and watched the birds flying free. Their freedom showed that there was something else beyond the loft, and – for the collier, beyond the pit. Yet he always went back there first thing Monday morning.

As for myself and my father, Jess, we enjoyed gardening more than pitching the horseshoe and pigeon racing. Besides which it brought in a little extra money especially if there were two of us at it. Although I first went gardening with my father when I was about seven years old. Often we'd weed, dig and tidy a gentleman's plot. But more often than not it would be a rectory garden and it was while we were working in the garden at Kimberley Rectory that I straightened up after a period of digging – looked towards the gate and saw a lean man standing there, sporting a ginger red beard. Two minutes later I found myself shaking hands with D.H. Lawrence although I had no idea he was a novelist until my father told me later. Now being a small boy I was quite naturally in awe of most grown men but David Herbert, as my father called him, was sporting this ginger red beard and looked almost like a prophet.

We sat beside a cluster of yew trees and the two men talked for a while. My father asked about the sales of David Herbert's first novel 'The White Peacock' and so far as I could make out they talked about books and colliers and little else. To tell you the truth I hadn't a clue to what or whom they were referring. It was all men's talk to me but I was still fascinated by Lawrence's red beard and studied it as they talked.

After about twenty minutes they stood up and shook hands, David Herbert saying 'Goodbye Jess' and then goodbye to me. Then, when he had gone down the path, I asked by father who he was and he replied to the effect that David Herbert Lawrence was a very clever man who could write novels, poetry, and speak three languages fluently.

He was, or had been, working as a teacher. Well I never saw Lawrence again and so far as I can make out neither did my father although he did once mention that David Herbert had trimmed his beard and had by then a neat moustache.

When Eastwood was throbbing with the news that Lawrence had eloped with Freida, the wife of Professor Weekley who taught at Nottingham University College, my father happened to say that as a boy the author had preferred playing with the girls instead of lads of around his own age and as if to make everyone aware of this, the lads used to chant

Dickie Dickie Denches
Plays. with the wenches
whenever they saw David Herbert walking down the street.

But after the elopement, Lawrence's name was mentioned daily in Eastwood where some people argued the fact that he was a very clever and talented man while others criticised his poems, stories and painting with a reverence that suggested they were jealous and pursuing Lawrence every artistic mood for the sheer purpose of making him seem foolish and in some ways, banal.

One man for whom everyone had respect was local businessman William Hopkin who was also Justice of the Peace and wrote a weekly column for the

Eastwood and Kimberley Advertiser. Hopkin had a shoe shop on Nottingham Road but I think his father took it over and William went to work at the post office next door. When his father died Hopkin moved back into the shoe shop and it was about this time he founded the Eastwood and District Ramblers club; I think it was called.

William and his wife Sally lived in a fine house on Devonshire Drive. Lawrence used to visit the house when he was a young man for here Eastwood's group of 'young' progressives used to meet. I think Hopkins died in 1951 and if you go into the Eastwood Public Library today you'll find a room bearing his name and in it are Lawrence's first editions and various letters.

My goodness, the community spirit in Eastwood was marvellous when I was living there as a young man. The shops were more like social clubs because everybody knew everybody else who went in. Mind you there was some gossip went on as you can well imagine but we chaps just ignored all this and went about talking greyhounds, darts, football and the young ladies we wouldn't have minded taking out if we did but have the money. I can remember a shop with arch shaped windows, Cullens London House I think it was called and then up by Hopkins shoe shop there was a pork butcher's shop managed, or perhaps owned, by Charlie Parker. The Parker family they managed their own cinema in Eastwood. This was situated near the Sun Inn and the old market place. Another cinema, on the main street called Nottingham Road, had a sign up outside so that you could hardly miss the Eastwood Empire.

Mind you I used to think it looked a bit shabby outside. There was litter on the pavements and posters torn on the billboards although they did smarten it up a bit at one time. It was built after my time; the Eastwood Empire. A man called F.G. Stubbs founded it in 1913. And I should think ninety per cent of the entire community visited it soon after it opened.

I remember sitting there in the dark watching silent actors and actresses gyrating about on the screen and thinking 'isn't technology a marvellous thing'. But of course it's nothing compared with today although you could get a good evening's entertainment there for twopence or threepence and it was open two or three evenings each week and again at the weekends.

Books; you could borrow from the Mechanics Institute and I think the Eastwood Conservative club stood next door.

One event that we always looked forward to was Teddy Rayner's Travelling Theatre. You had to pay tuppence to get a seat inside though. There were all kinds of plays put on in the big tent that was erected on a piece of flat ground alongside the Sun Inn.

Places of worship were the Methodist Chapel and the Eastwood Congregational Church. This was a very open and light type of building and I remember the lettered sign over the organ which read 'O worship the Lord in the beauty of holiness'.

In the market place, you could buy anything, you know. Cotton, lace, flowers, books. And none of the local women would buy at the advertised price if they could haggle and save a farthing or two here and there. Oh aye. You had to haggle if you wanted to survive in my younger days.

On Friday and Saturday evenings, most of the colliers gathered in the bar of The Three Tuns. I've drunk myself into a stupor there quite a few times in the past. And when you went for your beer you passed, or overtook, other men making for their favourite pub and heard pianos tinkling from the sing song sessions that were held in the parlours of some of the houses whose front doors opened straight out onto the street.

Beside the pub and cinemas, there was the billiard hall and often people would gather to listen to an evangelist orating from his soap-box in the market place. Yes. You never went out without meeting somebody or seeing something of interest whether it was a cow standing on the tramlines gazing at an oncoming tram or one of the Meakin family leading a young shire horse by the halter to the stables attached to Hill-Top House for the Meakins used to break in young shire horses for the farmers and carters hereabouts.

Sometimes we'd just lean on the railway bridge and watch the steam trains coming by or sit beside the gangs of young men who played marbles in the gutter of whichever street they happened to have been walking along. And as anyone used to say when he or she was referring to times gone by; 'Those were the days'. Happy, yes, but bloody hard for a working class lad like myself. Yet I wouldn't have lived anywhere but Eastwood or Kimberley where everybody you met on the pavement asked how you were with a sincerity that you seldom find anywhere in these days of hustle and bustle.''

ASPECTS OF MANSFIELD AND MANSFIELD WOODHOUSE

When I met him in an old people's home, Jim, a long retired collier, was undergoing a spell of convalescence following his third heart attack. Although looking forward to eating a meal and sipping a glass of water placed upon the table before him, Jim was eager to talk about Mansfield , 'the ancient town in Sherwood Forest' where he was born.

"Well, the first thing that springs to mind is walking up the side of Rock Hill, and my dad stopping me to show me a group of shack fronts, with doors and windows that had been fitted up against variously shaped outcrops of rock.

These were once lived in by the town's destitute families and I remember my dad saying that all you needed was a few willing hands, some wooden boards, hinges, panes of glass, hammer, nails, pick and shovel and you had all the necessary items for moving yourself into a Rock House.

I think there might have been only one family living there when I was a lad, but in some ways they looked like proper-houses from the outside. There was glass in the windows and at least one had a good porch fitted at the front. A bit like the storm porches you see today.

I expect they were dark and damp inside though, for I know of nothing colder than rock in winter. Mind you, they'd have the old fire going. I know some lads who used to hang around the railway sidings and stand on the bridges waiting for the trains to come in loaded with coal and coke.

When there was nobody about they used to stand on one another's shoulders up the side of the track, like a human pyramid, and the one at the top of course he'd be handed a bag which he'd fill with as many pieces of coal and coke as he could hold, then he'd hand it down and the lads would help him to the ground as the pyramid disbanded.

Often, of course, these 'coal nickers' as they used to call them were seen and pursued by the local bobby who after blowing his whistle ran after them brandishing a truncheon. Oh aye, it was like watching a Buster Keaton or Will Haye film if you happened to be walking near the railway some days; and more especially in winter. Well, I think the Rock Houses got their fuel that way, as well as begging it off the timber merchants and tree fellers. Anyway, they evidently survived. There was one family my dad told me about called the Chamberlains, and they reckoned to have been associated with the Rock Houses for about a hundred and fifty years.

They were besom makers, the Chamberlains, and their day began with a group of them walking out to what was then called 'Ling Forest', which was part of the old Sherwood Forest, but where ling and gorse thrived instead of oaks and pines. Once the ling had been gathered it was weathered for a year, then the Chamberlains and their neighbours the Smiths made the annual supply of besoms which they sold for fourpence-halfpenny each. One local historian went to the trouble of discovering that the ling and birch twigs were weathered in the garden of the Methodist Manse, which I think, was called Birchling House.

The birch branches and twigs were much sought after by the Smiths who sold them in wired-together bunches to the officers of the Mansfield Police Station who used them for punishing vandals and petty criminals -so they say. Both my dad and the school teacher told me how Mansfield sought recognition under the Parliaments Improvement Act that was passed in 1823. Once that was under way forty commissioners were elected to establish the town as a business centre, and it gained borough status about seventy years later, around 1891, I think it was.

If you buy a book or postcard depicting the Mansfield of eighty odd years ago you are looking at the town that I knew as a boy. The streets were busy with market traders lugging their wares on a barrow, back of a dray or pony and trap. Women buying meat, butter and lard at the corner shop. Boys and girls playing tin lurky and hide and seek in the church and pub doorways, and youths wheeling their sit up and beg bicycles over the cobblestones as they went to meet their mates and have a game of darts. Or perhaps they'd go for a day's fishing to Kings Mills Reservoir.

My grandfather, now he was the one you should be talking too. Goodness me he walked my little legs off around Mansfield and he knew the history like the back of his hand. The first time he took me out we walked together up Leeming Street, and I remember shutters being pulled across the shop windows because it was so hot and lads in shirt-sleeves wheeling their bicycles up the hilly thoroughfare, or freewheeling down the opposite side of the road. There was a few early cars about I think, and trams and the inevitable pony and gig and horses and carts. We went past Leckenby's Cafe that day as we did most days when we walked to town, and you can ask any old timer about Leckenby's in the First World War, because it was from their upper storey windows that the soldiers from Clipstone Camp used to throw cream cakes down at the local girls, to make them look up at the windows and the grinning faces of the young soldiers, some of whom attempted to make a date; but whether they were lucky or not; well that's a different story.

There was no gigantic Tesco in those days, but you passed corner shops that sold almost every type of household goods you could think of, saddlers' shops, harness makers, ironmongers, plumbers, glaziers and every week we joined the queue to file into Tom Sandersons, the tripe butchers.

In the early part of the century, there was a flour merchant business still operating in Mansfield, and I remember my grandad stopping outside the Swan Hotel and pointing to a stone, that I've passed a thousand times since, bearing the inscription – 1584. Mind you, the Swan was the oldest building on Church Street. When I was at senior school our teacher took us a walk down to it one afternoon.

He told us that the oldest parts of the building had been largely influenced by architects of the Tudor period and that some restoration work had been carried out in 1910, when the main archway was included into the new structure of the building.

When we had been standing outside listening to our teacher for a few minutes an old collier came hobbling up on his walking stick and said 'Look, you can see I'm in no hurry so I'll show you something really interesting if you come closer to the archway'.

And so we followed him and gathered round in an unruly manner, until our teacher divided us into groups, then each group went to the archway and the old man pointed along the brickwork with the end of his walking stick, and you could see the scratch marks where the wheel hubs of coaches and horse drawn vehicles had chaffed against the inner wall when a drivers judgement had proven to be a little offset.

Mind you, I should think some of the drivers were the worst for drink whenever they trundled a coach and four out of the stableyard by the Swan Hotel. A pagoda-shaped lamp was once hung over the archway so that a driver could drive his team through in the early winter darkness without any problems, but then I'll tell you another interesting thing.

Many years ago when workmen were restoring some tiles on the roof they discovered that splints of deer antler had been used to peg the tiles into the beams and the timber framing beneath. So what kind of craftsman put them there, eh? And was it once a Woodhouse or meeting place for wardens of Sherwood Forest before it was turned into a coaching inn and what have you?

I read somewhere that in the 1820s there were eight daily coach services setting out from the Swan Hotel. The coaches and four left for such destinations as Halifax, Leeds, Chesterfield, Lincoln, York, Derby and Gainsborough. Nottingham was on the schedule with five trips each day and you can imagine, can't you, the business deals that took place between the blacksmiths, saddlers, tack merchants and wheelwrights. My grandfather used to set up a skittling for a pig stall at the local horse fair which was officially opened as the Mansfield Carters Association Show. His two side-shows, skittling for a pig and pitching the horseshoe, were both profitable sidelines at that particular event anyway.

And did you know that Mansfield once had its own Gooseberry Pork Pie Fair where everybody ate sizeable portions of the sweetmeat? Oh aye! And both fairs were held on the piece of land that was once known as the Water Meadows.

There was a workhouse, too. A place where vagrants, the elderly and the unemployed were housed. Its address was 105 Stockwell Gate, and if anybody was criticizing somebody because they kept moving from one job to another they'd end by saying 'if you're not careful you'll finish up at 105'.

The knife and scissor grinder man – as they used to call him was named Mr Thrall, but my grandfather reckons everybody used to call him 'Throstle, Owd Throstle Thrall'.

Now 'throstle' is the name the old Victorian/ Edwardian countryman used to give to the song thrush which whistles from its songpost about nine or ten months of the year. So whether Owd Throstle Thrall was so named because he was a compulsive whistler is hard to say, although when I think back I reckon the whistling sound could also have emanated from the wet stones, which he used for sharpening, for these were driven by a belt and foot treadle.

I mentioned Leeming Street a while ago. Well, the Victoria Hall Theatre was there in my father's day, and also when I was a little lad. They staged everything there, Plays, Music Hall Nights, Opera, and every Christmas we were taken to an indoor circus. And when you walked along the streets you knew, you often heard piano's tinkering away behind the closed doors. Sometimes you'd hear a family standing around singing, and if anybody wanted sheet music, or to buy a musical instrument or even a piano, they could go to see the old chap who ran his music business from the shop premises on the corner of Toothill Lane.

Now Toothill Lane wasn't called that for nothing either. It was an exceptionally busy little street with pony traps and gigs, workhorses and dreys and butcher and baker boys making their deliveries on bicycles with big bar-sided baskets stuck on the front. But the tooting was done by the trams, because lads would be wheeling their bikes across the tramlines and if a tram was approached, the driver, or it might have been the conductor, either rang a bell or sound out a round of 'toot toots' on the hooter. And that's how my grandfather reckoned Toothill was given its name!'' *(Editor's note: 'Toot Hill' often denotes a burial mound, so its origin may be older!)*

Potato pickers, about 1920. (Photograph: F.Parkes)

MANSFIELD WOODHOUSE

''Another place I loved to explore was Mansfield Woodhouse, I think because it retained much of its past, and due to a combination of names, adequately-kept records and strong associations with Sherwood Forest.

Woodhouse as you probably know signifies a place in the forest where the vendorers and wardens used to meet. Some notes that I made from *Whites Nottingham Directory* published in 1841 described it as a parish with 1,871 inhabitants and 2,860 acres of enclosed land. But the boundary ended another twelve hundred acres beyond the settlement itself, and this White recorded as being 'the open forest of Sherwood'.

"But in my young days it was already a suburb of Mansfield. A small maze of streets with corner shops, carters' stables, bill boardings, tripe butchers and a fish and chip shop. However we were soon transported into the past whenever we went to look at Wolfhunt House, which was lived in at the time, but I remember how we used to stand and stare from the pavement opposite and imagine it as the sort of cobble and rubble shanty it once must have been. Now of course you would hardly tell it apart from any other house, because it has been modified several times. But in the reign of King John a wolfhunter lived on the site and his name was Vivarri. He was employed under Royal Warrant to rid the surrounding countryside of wolves.

The strange thing is, though, he was not allowed the use of a long bow, because it was thought he might bring down the occasional deer. So he had to close in on his quarry and use an axe or sword. I remember reading somewhere, that he had with him a band of young lads who lead greyhounds through the glades and a stronger breed of mastiff-type hound that could quickly despatch a wolf if the greyhounds turned it in the mastiff's direction.

Anyway, over the years Vivarri was succeeded by other wolf hunters, and in the reign of Henry IV the house was structurally strengthened to a style befitting a gentleman carrying the title of Sir Robert Plumpton, none-the-less. And he still had to retain the long withheld tradition of blowing a horn at sunset with the hope that it would drive way all the existing wolves.

Mind you, I don't suppose be blew the horn himself. He would have had one of his servants do it. But the horn blowing tradition was maintained for many years after Sir Robert moved in. I don't know who lives at Wolfhunt House now. I know Samuel Housley did at one time, but that would be in my great grandfather's time I reckon!''

Before he hinted to me that he was becoming tired, and would soon be ready for his afternoon nap, Jim mentioned visiting the Manor House once lived in by the late Major Rooke who died there in 1906. A keen historian, Major Rooke gained local fame by measuring and estimating the height and measuring the width of some quite sturdy oak trees in Sherwood Forest, the Major Oak being, of course the most prominent among them. According to Jim, this same gentleman also discovered the site of a Roman Villa consisting of seven rooms, with newly pointed walls and a Mosaic pavement, composing of red, yellow, white and grey tessera.

So for the local historian there is still much of interest to be found in and around the towns of Mansfield and Mansfield Woodhouse. My talk with Jim endorsed this fact and furnished me with a vein of curiosity that will, I hope, persuade me soon to return.

WILDLIFE ON THEIR DOORSTEPS

One summer in the mid-seventies, I visited an old people's home in Mansfield. Here I met a lady who had once lived with her husband and two children in a cottage beside the River Meden. The cottage can be seen today as one travels the road from Ollerton to Edwinstowe. Its approach road is a narrow lane leading directly down to the water meadows. In their early days together the family shopped in Edwinstowe sometimes catching the two-hourly bus or cycling with carrier bags dangling from the handlebars.

Eventually the husband acquired a small saloon car and travel became much easier. Trips to Nottingham and Mansfield, which had once been regarded as a luxury, could be arranged several days in advance according to the need and season. They were also able to explore Derbyshire's Peak District and the North Yorkshire Moors.

While the house was relatively snug and warm it was often damp in the winter, particularly when fog shrouded the fields. However, when she was in the house alone, the lady enjoyed the company of a dog and cat. There were also a few free range hens in the paddock and a pony, which her daughter rode at the weekends and during the long summer evenings.

"We were all fond of animals," she said, then recalled lying in bed beside her husband at night listening to the calls of moorhens and coots ferrying between the reedstalks of the river, that meandered close to the house.

"We used to hear the strange 'Ank Ank' calls of the herons too and watch them flying above the water or settling in the oaks and alders, so that they could digest their food and preen their feathers.

My word it's a strange sound to be heard in the night is the cry of the heron. But we got used to it just as we got used to everything else. You'd get mallard, lapwings and snipe come close to the house. Skylarks seemed to be singing all day long in the summer. We used to see a lot of linnets too.

Rabbits were everywhere. There were any number of warrens about the area and if poachers or trappers came with long nets, guns, dogs and ferrets it never seemed to make any difference to their numbers. We had a vixen visit us regularly although she would never bring the cubs. But we knew she had a litter in the hedgebanks between the cottage and the main road.

We used to be standing talking to the pony at sunset then see her loping down the fields; putting up the lapwings and rabbits and stopping now and again to scent ahead of her. She knew there would be a plateful of kitchen scraps on the forecourt and when she was feeding, she allowed the cat to come on one side and the dog on the other.

It was lovely to see the three of them together. But there came a day in the early autumn when I was drawn to the cottage windows by the hullabaloo going on outside. What I saw made my stomach turn. There was the vixen running down the fields towards the cottage with a pack of hounds in full cry at her tail. I was hoping she would come inside the house or go into one of the outbuildings but she turned to the hedgerows and began running along looking for a gap to get through. And do you know I think the earth stopper must have come along a few hours before and blocked off the runs used by the rabbits, hares and foxes.

Anyway this little vixen knew her end had come because as the hounds closed in on her she started squealing and chattering. Oh, it was terrible to hear her. Then there were men and horses everywhere watching the hounds mobbing around their kill.

Well I was so upset I got my husband to write to the landlord and try to get the hunt banned from entering the land. And we were successful. But though we occasionally glimpsed a fox some distance away, we never got on the same terms with them and if nothing else we 've kept that little fox alive in our minds, ever since that terrible day the hounds came in and killed her within yards of the house.

Deer were also regular visitors to the fields. Fallow deer. They used to come from the woods near Thoresby Colliery, cross the main roads and graze the fields in the early morning and again at dusk. They were mainly does with their fawns and yearlings and we reckoned they were the descendants of the deer that used to roam the woods of the Thoresby estate.

Yes. If anyone asks me about living in the Meden valley I forget all the days of teeming rain or screening blizzards and think of those sunset evenings spent in the paddock talking to our pony with rabbits gambolling around and between twelve and twenty fallow deer grazing fifty or sixty feet away.

Now that's really what you'd call living in the country.''

Fallow deer in October, with buck issuing his challenge to rivals (A.K. Smith)

While employed as a Countryside Ranger in the eighties, I met a lady who had once lived at the lodge gate entrance, which separates the Thoresby estate from the National Trust owned property of Clumber Park.

The lodge is actually inside the Clumber boundary and the long tract of woodland fringing the two estates is known as the Thoresby Border.

With two young children about the place, a working husband coming home to his meals, and a dog and cat to keep an eye on when everyone else was out of the house, this lady found life as a fifties housewife quite fulfilling, but she was always aware of the variety of woodland birds that visited the garden birdtable.

In the summer, the surrounding glades and thickets provided a habitat for such summer visitors as the spotted flycatcher, blackcap and garden warbler; and they still do today. Clumber is also popular for playing host to all three species of woodpecker, a surprising number of nuthatches and the occasional family group of tree-creepers.

The family at the lodgehouse kept a bird book on a shelf close to one of the windows and, by regularly referring to it, were soon able to identify the different species of titmice and finches that visited the garden.

"Except when it was raining or snowing, it was always pleasant accompanying the children to school. We had to walk our cycles over the bridge spanning the River Poulter, than ride along the parkland drives to the main lodge gates where we sometimes exchanged pleasantries with the keeper's wife. From there, we'd cycle the half mile or so of road, with Forestry Commission woodland on one side and water meadows the other,'' the lady volunteered.

Her children were first educated at the little school house situated on the Carburton crossroads. It is perhaps worth noting here that the schoolhouse was reputed to have been the smallest in England.

While crossing the Poulter bridge, the mother and her two children would often pause to watch the waterfowl in the reeds and backwaters below, and it was here one day that they sighted a fine dog otter.

It was hunting through the reeds with its muzzle close to the vegetation; exploring a backwater islet unaware that the three people were watching from the parapet above. To add further to their delight, they saw the otter submerge and swim in the pools around the bridge buttresses before it reappeared on the opposite side and swam, with head above the surface, toward the small weir and the Chapel stretch of the river.

Most of the Dukeries lakes and rivers were still providing habitat for a few otters in the 1950s and the lady had recollections of hearing the whistles of a dog otter piercing the silence of a moonlit night in the early spring.

Autumn also brought another sound within earshot of the lodgehouse for September and October is the rutting season of the red deer. Quite a number of these fine animals were then populating the woodlands and forestry plantations of the Thoresby Border.

Believed to have descended from the park strain of Sherwood Forest red deer, which were once enclosed at Welbeck, the mature stags were sizeable beasts and more than one keeper's cottage between Carburton and Thoresby displayed a mounted head or rack of antlers on the wall, for a tally had to be maintained of just how many deer there were in the neighbourhood, due to the fact that acres of the original Sherwood Forest country were undergoing a replanting programme, and red deer, in particular, can do considerable damage to plantings of young saplings.

It was therefore necessary to keep the numbers down by culling. The stags, when they could be located through tracking, were shot in September and the hinds which roamed through the woodland tracts of the Thoresby estate, in December. Therefore there was venison on the tables of one or two of the remote cottages during these times, as well as in the kitchens of such great houses as Thoresby and Welbeck.

The Duke of Newcastle shot a fine stag on the Welbeck estate in 1929 and presented the head to the Nottingham natural history museum. Other heads graced the banqueting halls, billiard rooms and private libraries used by the gentry.

In the early 1950s the Forestry Commission rangers and estate gamekeepers worked together on their deer culls. Usually a keeper was perched in the boughs of a tree with a shotgun alongside him and the selected stag or hind driven in his direction by a line of beaters. My informant recalls that, on one occasion, the gamekeeper only succeeded in wounding his quarry which attempted to gore him when he stepped into the glade, where the animal had been brought down by his shot.

Once the September cull was over peace returned to the glades and thickets and the family at the lodgehouse liked nothing better than to stand in the garden on a frosty October night listening to the deep, far-carrying roars of the stags as they roamed through the woods in search of hinds.

"I remember those sounds the instant I think of the times when we used to live on the Thoresby border.

We woke to mornings of birdsong, heard the occasional otter calling down by the river but it was the roars of the stags that used to send a shiver along my spine, for our Saxon and Norman ancestors must have heard stags roaring in the forest of long ago and somehow as we stood there in the night blackened garden, we could sense the connection between the past and the present."

"The Archers"

The late Joe Archer of Wighay Wood lived alone there in a cabin built with his own hands. I first met Joe when I was walked the circuitous route from Greasley and across the Misk Hills to Wighay. With Annesley Hall and Moorgreen still to traverse the group of walkers which I was leading, were obliged to stop and have a word with Joe whose presence we were unaware of, until he appeared from a rough wooden gate that had been fixed into the hedge row bordering Wighay Wood.

Whenever he heard people on the footpath Joe always opened the gate and immediately asked them the time. He used this ruse to introduce himself and strike up a conversation. Frankly I am glad that he did because this enabled me to learn something about the man who had lived as 'a solitary' from the age of nine and survived admirably until he was eighteen, when he enlisted for service with the Army and eventually became a regular.

"We Archers lived in a little tumbledown house in Hucknall. I was one of a family of nine. Like many, my generation I learnt more from talking to farriers, ploughmen and poachers than I did from attending school and although I was something of a loner by nature, I was governed by a mischievous streak which turned me into a practical joker.

I loved to see the family disorganised through some prank I'd played on them. But one day, when I was about nine, my dad grabbed hold of me by the collar and set about me. He was so angry that he just about knocked the living daylights out of me then, when he was through, he opened the front door and told me to get out of the house and never come back.

And I did just that. I began by eating berries and a poacher's boy gave me a knife, so I used to take potatoes, swedes and carrots out of the soil, clean them in one of the streams, collect kindling and cook them over a fire.

I used old discarded biscuit tins as roasting tins and kept them washed and stowed away in certain sheltered thickets and I slept out in the woods around Wighay and Annesley when the weather was good and bedded down in ditches and hays tacks during the uncertain nights in the spring and autumn.

When the winter was with us I'd wait till it was dark and then creep up into the loft of a barn or a stable in one of the several farmyards around here and I don't believe anyone knew I existed except the local poachers. These people – the poaching families of Hucknall, Greasley and Moorgreen -were very good to me. They gave me their children's cast off clothing, old pit boots and trenchcoats then took me out into the fields and along the hedgebanks to study the ways of the rabbit so I could get a ready supply of fresh meat.

Oh aye. I'd set my first snare by the time I was ten. And I caught my first rabbit. Bless 'im! When I'd got a few skins together I used to sell them to a furrier in Hucknall and make a few pence that I spent on extra food. By the time I was seventeen I looked like a wild man, with long hair and a beard. I'd also got so used to sleeping out, that whenever I went into a poacher's house it felt claustrophobic.

But then war broke out and even the poaching families found food in short supply. I realised that there would be no old clothes and cast off boots simply because the men of my age were enlisting or getting called up. So I thought 'to hell with it' – I'll do the same. I passed my medical and for the first time in my life was given a suit to wear and a pair of good, hardwearing boots for the parade ground. These I treated as if they were gold.

Well I'd not had any schooling to speak of so I was only given a choice of what I could do. They were cook, or officer's batman – basically, a flunkey; I chose to be one of these and, do you know, those officers I served under were absolute gentlemen.

I used to press their trousers, iron their shirts, bull up their boots, and webbing belts ready for the parades. I'd got my own little bedroom, a bed, cupboard and locker for my personal belongings, and my army gear. Yes, I was one of the few who considered himself fortunate. Most of the others couldn't wait to get back home. But I signed on for twenty years.

Anyway, I did get demobbed eventually and I remember coming back to Nottinghamshire, getting off the train at Hucknall station and thinking, 'Where am I going to live, now?'. I was unable to trace my brothers and sisters because something held me back. But I went to look if the old house was still there and found it reduced to rubble. Whether the street had been hit by a bomb or not I never found out. Instead I just picked up me suitcase and set off up the road had a meal in a little café then walked up to Wighay. I slept rough for two or three nights, left my overcoat and suitcase in the hollow of a tree then scoured the area for planks of wood and built my first cabin beside the stream in Wighay Wood.

Over the years I enlarged it. Sometimes I snared a few rabbits and pheasants then swapped them with a local timber merchant so that I could get the planks and posts I wanted. I slept on the floor of that cabin and used dry sacks for bedding. One day a lorry pulled up in the lane beside the wood and two men got out. "Pile of wood for you from the timber-yard, Joe. It won't cost you anything except a smile," said one of the men. And smile I certainly did. I couldn't help it!

Within two weeks, I'd built the cabin you see today. Then I went down to Hucknall, and swapped a brace of pheasants for a tin of creosote and brush. A week later I was back with another brace and two or three hares. And on that occasion I brought back with me a roll of tarpaulin, tin of tacks and a hammer.

By the time the autumn had set in I had a secure roof over my head. My food I lifted from the land. Potatoes, parsnips, mangols, cabbages, kale, blackberries, raspberries, apples, rabbits, hares and pheasants. Most of it I cooked outside on a kindling fire, using biscuit tins, or anything I could get hold of, as roasting tins and pans.

Just like people became beachcombers I became a ditch scourer. Yes it's quite amazing what you find discarded and thrown into ditches. Especially near farms. I came across two or three quite good buckets that way. When the Spring came I got enough wood to make myself a table and one or two chairs.

There was no electricity of course so I bought candles and a box or two of matches. When the darkness came I was alone with my thoughts; my memories.

And all night long you could hear the stream rippling and chuckling its way between the stones. Yes it's a happy stream; the one that comes through Wighay Wood.

In what little spare time I had, I became an observer of wildlife. My poacher's instinct had long taught me the ways of ground game but I began to watch the woodland birds. I'd memorize their shape and colours and walk down to Hucknall library and see if I could find pictures of them in the nature books.

I couldn't read half the names though, so the librarian used to help me. She'd talk to me steadily as if I was a child. I learnt quite a bit from her and the other members of staff. They should have been social workers because they were really nice understanding people.

There was a pair of Canada geese used to come down to roost on Annesley lake and graze the scrubland around the lake too. A pair of great-crested grebe used to nest on the partly-submerged alder and willow branches, and there were always a few roach or tench in the water.

Through my rabbiting activities, I got to know the land contours round here pretty well. Besides rabbits there are a few badgers and foxes. Badgers you had to sit out for long into the dusk but foxes you'd glimpse in broad daylight.

Some winter nights I used to sit in the glow of the candle lit cabin listening to the wind whining between the tree branches. Then, as often, as not a vixen would begin skirling and screaming from somewhere along the stream bank. A blood curdling sound that and although I knew what it was it still made my hair stand on end every time I heard it.

I still hear the occasional vixen yelling in the midwinter darkness and also the dog foxes barking across the fields. Badgers though, well I've seen the occasional one laying dead by the roadside, visited their setts and followed their paths across country but I've never seen a badger in broad daylight, more is the pity.

For the last two or three summers, a magnificent fallow buck has been grazing the fields around Wighay, I've seen him in the glades and rising from the bracken fronds. But I like best to see him in August and September when his antlers are fully formed and he's filled out in the neck and body, in readiness for the autumn rut.

When you begin to realise there's a nip in the air it also occurs to you that the buck's gone off to the doe territories, around the Forestry plantations and the hills closer to Annesley Hall. But unless you go out walking that way you don't see him until the following April, just after he has cast his antlers.''

I asked Joe if he'd ever been asked to move from Wighay Wood.

Such fine red deer stags as this roamed at will throughout 'The Dukeries

"No. I can honestly say that no one's ever bothered me. I believe Wighay is part of the Annesley Park estate but neither the landowner nor his agent has ever suggested I move on, although they must know I'm here because I'd had the keepers drop me in a brace of pheasants or partridges from time to time.

One youth who I met here on the footpath brought a sackful of potatoes he'd carried on his back from Hucknall and wouldn't let me pay a penny towards them.''

Joe was literally surrounded by animals for, as I stood looking at the weekly washing spread out to dry on the cabin roof, a host of cats and kittens came over to be petted and there were four first-cross mongrel dogs each chained to a post close to the cabin door.

The dogs barked and strained when they saw a stranger on their territory and it was obvious they were in fine fettle. However, although I had my reservations about Joe keeping them chained, I never made this known to him.

Joe, incidentally, was retired when I first met him. He regarded his state pension as 'an absolute luxury'. Among his few other luxuries were two paraffin heaters, which he had been given by well wishers who called infrequently to see him.

On our last meeting, he decided to walk into Hucknall and collect a can of paraffin for it was a bitterly cold day with every tree branch, twig and fencepost coated with hoar frost. Although lacking an overcoat, he was wearing a lovatt suit, heavy army type boots; and socks and a scarf 'knitted especially for me, by a lady from the church.' At the end of the lane we shook hands and went our separate ways. Joe to Hucknall, myself to Annesley.

A host of commitments prevented me from walking the Greasley Annesley footpaths for many years but, sometime around 1988, Joe died at his house in the woods. Like many people I was not aware of his passing until I read the brief write up that appeared in the local paper.

In the personal obituaries which followed he was described as both 'a true gentleman' and 'unforgettable character', and to add to these I knew Joe to have possessed a courageous spirit which induced him to live by his wits. Nor did he accept a handout from the State until it was due and while he found occasional companionship among those who came to see him, he was happiest when he was with animals, and observing wild life in particular.

It was through my own obsession with wildlife that I chanced to meet Jim, a warrener employed by the Forestry Commission and also the late Eric Spafford who, with his wife Margaret, lived in a delightful house within the grounds of the Rufford Abbey estate.

Jim also lived in a delightful cottage where on Saturday morning, visits with my son, we talked about foxes, badgers, deer, woodland birds and ground game. His garden looked out over the fields. In a paddock close to the house a sandy pony was sometimes kept – perhaps in need of company. It soon got the habit of stretching its neck over the hedge and removing the washing from the line. Jim soon put me in touch with the forest fox earths and badger setts where I sometimes sat out until after dark and had some memorable experiences with a vixen and her well-grown cubs.

We watched chiffchaffs and willow warblers, woodpigeons and pheasants. Along one of the forest rides was a static tank which was visited by a pair of moorhens. These birds, we concluded, had probably nested high in one of the many pines and although moorhens frequent some quite narrow streams and ditches we were surprised to learn that the pair were tenanting a water tank surrounded by barbed wire and installed during the last war.

Wherever time permitted, Jim drove out with us in a Landrover, from which we observed wheatears displaying on ploughland close to Winkburn Hall, a pair of little ringed plovers feeding around the edges of a drinking pool for cattle and a cuckoo flying alongside the vehicle, as we drove along the lanes near Maplebeck.

My encounters with wildlife were further enriched by rambling the forest trails with my late friend, Eric Spafford. We tramped through miles of pine forest and heathland in search of such secretive birds as nightjar and long-eared owl. We watched garden warblers in the glades of The Birklands, admired the masses of bluebells, and heard an occasional evening cuckoo, as we explored Cutts Wood.

But Eric's favourite occupation was making movie films of the local birds and mammals. I recall a lovely sequence of fox cubs romping together in the bracken fronds of Pittance Park for, while Eric filmed the cubs, the vixen sat on her haunches, watching Eric!

On another occasion, he discovered a pair of greater spotted woodpeckers rearing a family, in the cleft of a silver birch tree situated beside the mineral railway line in the Clipstone and Rufford Forest. Here he was rewarded by getting some quite memorable shots of bird behaviour photographed, of course, from a hide. From the same hide, both Eric and myself watched a family of kestrels being fed by the female as she returned with a vole to the hole in the trunk of a sizeable oak.

Living in a relatively remote position Eric and his wife Margaret often walked out into the forest to look for wildflowers or listen to tawny owls hooting from the hedgeside oaks at dusk. Like the other people mentioned in this chapter they never took a single day of their lives for granted and portrayed a spiritual calmness, that I find typical of those who live with wildlife around them.

MEETINGS WITH A NOTTINGHAMSHIRE POACHER

Mike the poacher lived 'out Blidworth way' and would divulge nothing more of his private address than that. I have met him twice. The first occasion was at Deerdale, situated on the edge of the Clipstone and Rufford Forest which is currently owned and managed by the Forestry Commission. The second was on a foray in winter hoar frost when I crossed Boothamsall Common and was walking down to where the rivers Meden and Maun converge, at a delightful spot known as Conjure Alders. Mike was by then retired and "keen to be abed at night rather than setting up long nets beneath the light of the moon". But on each occasion, we found a glade in which to sit, and, while sipping from a flask of coffee, I listened as he reminisced about his exploits in and around the coverts and private estates of North Nottinghamshire.

Brought up with the belief that if the lord of the manor could dine regularly on pheasant, so should everyone else, Mike had learned the ways of ground game – such as pheasants, partridges, hares and rabbits – before he left school.

His first rabbit was taken in a snare made entirely by his own hands when he was in his ninth summer! His father, grandfather, and great-grandfather were poachers. But his father had died when Mike was quite young, so he took on the responsibility of providing fresh meat for his mother and nine brothers and sisters.

"I was no good at school, although I tried my best because I didn't want to get strapped. But my mind was always somewhere else; along the hedges, ditches, and in the woods and spinneys. I was setting up snare wires in my head when the other kids were talking about Tom Mix and Laurel and Hardy.

I remember catching my first hare. The cows at the nearby farm were filing into the milking shed as I ran, half crouched like a Red Indian, past the outbuildings and down to the covert. Everywhere was white over with frost, but

I knew I'd got him before I saw him 'cause I could hear his back legs thumping into the ground.''

"There he was, trying to run with the noose still round his neck, and I had to watch those back legs because they were powerful and the toe-nails could lacerate your wrists. But I cuffed him in the neck the way I'd been shown, withdrew the pin and half-dragged and half-carried him home. My, I wasn't half proud of mi' little self, I can tell you!''

"There's another way of takin' a hare, although ideally you need an accomplice who's skilled at stalking and crawling. What you do is to find the hare lying in his daytime hollow, usually made in a furrow or in a field of deadened grasses, and one of you stays behind while the other walks a circuit and then stops some way off so that the hare can see you in his sideways vision.

The man then takes off his scarf and puts it on the ground. The hare is filled with curiosity while the accomplice is hopefully creeping up from behind.

The first man then removes his trilby or cap – as was the headgear usually worn by semi-professional fieldman like – puts it on top of the scarf, stands about singing or something, then takes off his long coat, folds it up and places it over the pile. By this time your quarry is pretty well transfixed with curiosity, and long before you have shed your jacket and waistcoat your mate has hopefully succeeded in creeping up, grabbing the hare by the ears and cuffing him at the back of the neck before he begins to kick out in self-defence.

Aye, I've had many a jugged hare taken in this way. But poaching is about listening, studying tracks, trails and signs. You must learn to walk softly and to crawl when necessary. You must also learn how to handle a ferret, and all the nets relevant to catching ground game. You must also own a purse net, long net and gate net.

A gate net is often best for a hare because if you study their runs across the fields you'll see that they frequently go under the bottom rung of a farm gate, so you set the net accordingly, leave your mate hidden behind the hedge, go to the far side of the field, then walk across it until the hare leaves its form and goes bounding down to the farm gate and into the net spread along and beneath the lower rung. Often, we were walking home with a couple of hares tied over our shoulders by the time the sun was rising between the trees.

In later years though, I drove a van, filled with dry sacks, but the gamekeepers were still suspicious and keen, and you'd only to pull in alongside a hedge that was part of the Welbeck or Thoresby, Estate and sit for five minutes studying the ground contours before a gamekeeper would appear, tap on the window and ask what you were doing!'

Woodsmen posing after felling a beech (Photograph: F.Parkes)

"Oh yes! They were very astute men, those Dukeries gamekeepers. But then again, so were we! We took care never to step out of the van, but before I was mobilised it was different, and difficult because you could tell a poacher or his ilk a mile off. Usually we wore corduroy trousers and a jacket and overcoat that was too big for us because we'd got special pockets for storing the odd partridge or rabbit sewn into the lining. That's how you get the name 'poacher's pocket'. Mind you, the mainstay of the poachers' profession used to be netting rabbits. At least until the myxomatosis outbreak put a stop to it."

"Being basically nocturnal, rabbits need to be flushed out of their burrows by ferrets. These members of the weasel family could usually be obtained from any of the mining communities. I've had the yellow ones, and the black and yellow polecat type ferrets, and the collier who was noted for selling them also offered to train them for rabbiting. This, though would have cost me another half-crown, because you could buy a ferret for one half-crown and have it trained for another half-crown, so ensuring that you'd spent at least five shillings.

Me? I always trained them myself. The basic secret is to keep your ferret fed but not overfed, otherwise he'll go to sleep in the rabbit warren and unless you've got him attached to a line you're either going to have to wait until he wakes or dig him out.

They're excitable animals, ferrets. Keep you fingers stiff when he's sniffing them because if they baulk you could get bitten. So you have to be calm, and either carry your ferret in a tight little sack or in your poacher's pocket.

If you want, you can always put a muzzle on your ferret to stop him killing the rabbits. Sometimes I used a line and collar. It just depended on how much time I had.

When he's in the warren, you put purse nets across the entrance and watch. The ferret may show before the rabbits. Or it may be a good fifteen to twenty minutes before you see either one of them. Ideally you should have a mate with you and be taking it in turns to keep an eye out for the gamekeeper. Sometimes I used to lie and listen into the warren because you could occasionally hear an old buck rabbit thumping with his hind legs. Often it's the doe rabbit or her babies that come out first, and when they show you turn the nets and cuff 'em at the back of the neck.

Bolder men than me carried a gun, and shot the rabbits that escaped. But the problem was the gamekeeper. He'd hear a gunshot a mile away and be on you in no time, or at least send his dogs in pursuit before he arrived himself. Rabbit nets are white when you first buy them. So what we used to do was rub sand, soil and mud across the cording so that it turned brown.

If the ferret failed to come out of the burrow when we'd got a satisfactory haul of rabbits, we used to set fire to a piece of sacking or a sprig of gorse and push it down the entrance hole – so that the fear of the smoke would turn him in the direction we wanted. We'd keep all the holes blocked except the one we intended the ferret to come out of, and he'd usually show in the end. Another method was to slit the belly of one of the rabbits we'd killed and push the dead animal around the tunnel in the hope that the ferret would come when he smelt the blood. At other times you could hold a blade of grass between your thumbs and blow onto it. The sound resembles the squealings of a trapped rabbit. Failing all that, you'd take a whin hoe and shovel and try to dig him out. I've lost four or five ferrets down rabbit warrens in the past. In fact, I remember us leaving two down a big warren on the Welbeck Estate because we spotted about four game keepers running hell for leather across the paddock towards us.

I used to really enjoy netting, thought. That's when you are holding one end of the net and your mate the other, and walking up a field while your terriers and lurchers send the rabbits and hare in all directions. But most of the burrow entrances we had blocked with nets beforehand, and so eventually the little furry runners would turn our way with the dogs after them and we caught them in the nets. Running out a long net, hanking it down with steel pins or wooden pegs is a skill in itself, and if I had one with me now I'd show you what I mean!''

Sadly, in his early days Mike had followed his grandfather's and father's example and used a gin trap, which was pegged into the ground and carried serrated jaws that snapped around the victim's leg once it had been triggered off.

Mike continued:

''Before going the rounds and checking what was in your snares, it was best to spend some time in a tree or thicket just looking and listening because now and again a gamekeeper came across the snare and waited in ambush. I might add that he was never alone, either. When we were out long netting we'd sometimes come across a 'covey' of partridges. Now, normally they weren't worth bothering with because we didn't make much money out of them. So, our wives made partridge pies. On the odd occasion that we indulged in illegal partridge shoots we'd have the dogs put them up before us. They roost on the ground, do partridges, among clovers or kale or deep tussock grass. In the darkness they sit together but with each bird facing outwards. If you're as clever a poacher as you think you are, then you can usually move in to them with the long net at the ready. But you'd already have to have looked the field over by daylight and memorized obstacles like tree snags or clumps of briar – anything that could hamper the flexibility of the net. You had to watch out for ewes and lambs as well blundering into the net.

Why, I remember one night, when we were netting the water meadows near Warsop. Within minutes I couldn't see my mate. All I could see was the grass at my feet and the fog in front of me. Then the long net started tugging and I began to haul it in. Oh dear! It was going all over the place and I thought, "What the devil is he doing?"

I shouted to him once or twice, but he didn't answer. Then I saw why; because through the fog came this great Dairy Shorthorn bull with one end of the net dangling from his horns. Boy, did I run!

Bugger the net! We had to put that down to experience. Or perhaps wear and tear would have been a better term. My mate? Oh, he'd taken off the minute he saw the bull, but he never said owt to me though! Said later he was so frightened he couldn't speak. And if he were here now I'd say, "Well speaking never bothered yer before or since!"

Sometimes we'd snare the pheasants and more than once we've hidden in a covert and put down dried peas threaded onto a length of cotton or very thin twine. When the birds were struggling with these, and found they were unable to swallow, we used to spring out and throw a net over them."

"I tell you, we've had bigger birds than pheasants in our day though. We've had poultry. But never from the little farmer, or someone who we knew to be badly off. Nay; it was the estate farmyards we visited. We'd crouch either side of the gateway then pour grain and chicken mash out of a sack and into a bowl. Then we poured whiskey over it all. Crikey! Have you ever seen a drunk turkey?"

We'd have hens, ducks, turkeys and guinea fowl staggering about on the ground in front of us like daft little old men. So we cuffed 'em, put 'em in a sack and away we went.

But the saddest, perhaps most despicable thing, I had to do was shoot two mute swans. I did it once, but I'd never do it again. But I had to do it; or let two or three families with young children down.

You see, it was at the time of the General Strike and people were hungry. I've seen 'em crying with hunger. Especially little children. I know it's hard to imagine, but it did happen. And one morning I said to these families, "Hang on throughout the day and I'll be back by nightfall with a sackful of pheasants."

Now I'd pin-pointed the Boothamsall coverts and Crow Park Woods in my mind because that year there were hundreds of wild pheasants ranging out that way. Anyway, I cycled with a bag on my shoulder and a gun in the bag, but when I got to Crow Park and Conjure Alders there wasn't a pheasant to be seen.

The Thoresby Estate keepers had either rounded them up or some of the old Ollerton poachers had got there before me.

No, there was nothing to be seen. Not even a mallard on the river. But then downstream came two mute swans. The male or 'cob' was a wildish bird and he surged over the current with his neck back and his wings beautifully arched over his back. I looked at the cob then thought of those little children back home crying because they were cold and hungry. So I said to myself -'It's either you or them, my friend!' – I'm afraid it was him. I put the body under the little bridge that goes over the Whitewater and cycled home.

'Fill the copper you use for washing the clothes in with hot water because you're going to have to boil a swan in it', I told the children's mother when I got to the village.

That night I cycled back to the Whitewater bridge and shot the cob's mate. Then, with two swans bulging in the sack tied across my back, I rode without lights down to my village as if the hounds of hell were after me. And they would have been if the gamekeepers had known what I'd done! But I can tell you now that two swans, plucked and dressed and boiled in a copper can feed three hungry families for a week!''

I interrupted Mike's natural flow of speech to ask him if he'd ever been caught while out poaching.

"Caught while out poaching? Oh yes, I've been to prison twice! Did a three-month stretch on each occasion. God, for a man who loves freedom the way I did it was pure hell. Purgatory, in fact! Yet you knew when you were out in the fields that someday the time would arrive. Poaching rabbits – which were really your bread and butter income – has sent more poachers to prison than any other form of poaching.

Monday morning in the dock with a burly policeman beside you is never the best of mornings to remember. 'Trespassing in pursuit of game. Found with two dead rabbits about your person. I fine you ten pounds, or alternatively you may serve three months' imprisonment.' I had to go to prison because I never had two fivers to rub together except when I'd just been to the game dealers – one of whom, I think, might have shopped me at least once.

When I had done my time the people in the village used to stop me and say: "Oh, I haven't seen you about for some time, Mike." And I'd say, 'No, well I've been down to the city working in the Queen's service.'

Never once did I refer to it as prison, although, by God, to a man like me it was! There's nothing so sure as that!'' Mike's accomplices were described by him in the way that one might describe a Walt Disney characterization.

"Well, there was Big Ben. Always a good man to be with, but if you were talking to him and walking uphill at the same time his speech would come sort of muffled, and when you glanced up at him you'd see that his head had become totally enveloped by cloud." And of Danny Kelly – "Danny Kelly? Well he was so small that he had to stand on tiptoe to look into a skylark's nest. It's a wonder he wasn't crushed to death under our boots. But he managed to survive somehow, did Danny Kelly."

The last time I met Mike at Boothamsall he said, "Oh, aye. Sometimes, you know, it pays you best to be regarded as the village idiot. I mean there was once a poacher who caught a mallard duck and sat plucking it by the riverside.

When he'd taken all but a few of the feathers from the carcass, the undergrowth crackled behind him and a dark shadow suddenly shut out the sun. Glancing up, the poacher saw the game keeper standing before him. At the same time, he threw the duck's carcass forward into the water. "Okay, Williams, I've got you this time!" boomed the keeper. "Got me now? What for?" the poacher asked.

"Taking a duck from the water and killing it!"

"Oh, I haven't killed it," said Williams. "It's there, look. I'm just looking after its clothes while it goes for a swim!"

A SCATTERING OF RECOLLECTIONS

HAY-MAKING DAYS

Elsie and Evelyn spent the early days of their childhood in a large stone house with concrete floors. Their father, a local businessman and landowner, decided one day to convert a large playroom of the house into a pork butcher's shop which, for many years, attracted regular custom from the immediate locality.

The nearby allotment gardens were turned into piggeries where domestic rabbits were also bred for the pot.

Besides his pork butchery business, the girls' father managed a cart, carriage and trap hire venture. He also owned several horses, which Elsie and Evelyn sometimes followed when the animals were taken from the stable and led through the streets of Basford to Bagnall Lane, where they turned right and proceeded up the steep lengthy incline of Broxtowe Lane, to the blacksmith and farriers shop known as Forge Cottage, which had been converted from the living quarters of the cottage situated on the corner of St Martins Lane, Strelley.

Here, until fairly recent times, a notice stood beside the fieldgate which indicated that there was to be 'NO RIDING ON THE FOOTPATHS. PENALTY IF CAUGHT; FORTY SHILLINGS'. Other trips into the surrounding countryside included a pony and trap ride up to the Broxtowe Inn close to Cinderhill and Nuthall, for this hostelry was owned by the girls' paternal grandfather who also owned most of the land extending from this inn to the Three Ponds public house.

Their grandfather spent little time on the land however but was usually to be found working in the cellars or behind the bar of his beloved Broxtowe Inn.

Many pub regulars of that time labelled him 'the most generous man in the district' and Evelyn, in particular, remembers that his generosity was extended to the local tramps and itinerants, none of whom he allowed to by-pass his premises until they had accepted his invitation to sit on a bench outside and be served with a cheese roll and a glass of ale.

Today, the past is commemorated by such events as the annual ploughing match

Every hay-making season, the sisters were conveyed up to their grandfather's fields by a pony and trap belonging to their father and there they helped position the stooks, did odd jobs around the stables or served the main workforce with cool drinks, cake and sandwiches.

Not surprisingly, the sisters loved riding in a trap being pulled by a trotting pony. The rear seat of a trap was apparently known as the 'Dickey' seat but for what reason, or how this name came about, neither of the ladies are sure.

"It was just taken for granted that if you sat in the back you were sitting in the Dickey seat. We never questioned it beyond that," Evelyn explained.

When they were not helping with the hay-making the girls spent long hours at the seemingly thankless task of potato picking. "I think I've been potato picking in every field between the Broxtowe Inn and The Three Ponds," said Evelyn when I visited her home quite recently.

Her sister Elsie's strongest countryside recollection revolved around her summers spent as a Girl Guide. Another of the girls' uncles allowed the guides to pitch bell tents, on the field that fronted his picturesque farmhouse which was set back on the right-hand side of Coventry Lane, as one approached the Balloon House crossroads with Strelley at their backs and Stapleford signposted ahead.

It should be remembered that, in the times to which we are referring, Coventry Lane was less than half the width that it is today and was known as Blackbird Lane, while the Balloon House crossroads was little more than four rough tracks converging alongside several small turnpike cottages.

Horses and ponies frequently grazed the undulating fields of Holly Bush Farm where Elsie and Evelyn played beside the source of that delightful stream that is still known to many as The Tottle Brook. When the guides were camping there the girls' uncle and aunt used to stroll over from the door of their farmhouse to check with the organisers that the arrangements were to their satisfaction while the girls cooked on small, yet fearsome, fires made from the kindle they had constantly to collect from the nearby ditches and hedgerows or the deeper woods.

Usually the camps lasted from Friday evening until after tea on Sunday and when the girls went back to school the following day they felt refreshed and eager to attempt each lesson as it was put before them. In fact, camping out of doors and learning to live from the land gave them an entirely new concept of the countryside – and life in general.

Footpath Over Ten Lands

Bob, who eventually became Evelyn's husband, was born in a house facing the mill at Mill Street, Basford. One of his favourite walks took him down High Street to Breffits Lane on Nuthall Road. This was part of the Colliers Pad that continued through Cherry Orchard to Radford Woodhouse but Bob turned off into the surrounding countryside with little thought of heading in that direction, because as a young boy he had discovered that by turning right across a tract of wide fields and meadows he could take the path that progressed steadily uphill to a stile, which gave the walker further access along the edge of the fields with Broxtowe Woods on the left and an occasional glimpse of the Hall rising solidly against a background of heavily foliaged trees. This area was known by many as Ten Lands which probably denoted the possibility of there being a total of ten fields used for cultivation and grazing cattle.

In one of these fields was a deep bell pit of which all the local walkers were apparently aware. From then on the path veered north in the direction of Bulwell and crossed more sloping fields to the rough bridge which took Bob and his friends over the Babbington Colliery railway line to a stile fixed between the hedgerow and a little walnut tree. After climbing the stile he found himself on the main Nottingham/Nuthall road facing The Broxtowe Inn where a warm welcome was extended to Bob and Evelyn in particular, due to her grandfather still being its overseer, landlord and owner.

The walk home along Nuthall Road reflected more of the industrious age the couple were living in for they saw colliers, hauliers and carters carrying or humping coal all around the wharves of Babbington Colliery and the colliers' wives and daughters hanging out their washing on the communal lines of such places as Cinderhill Square, Brickyard Cottages and Napoleon Square.

Reflecting for a moment upon the footpaths, Bob, like myself, believes that the majority go farther back in time than we often realise and although many originated due to local migrations by animal species that were hunted, like the deer and wild oxen, both he and I agree that quite a number of routes could have been pioneered by small groups of monks travelling from one place of worship to another. To illustrate this point Bob further pointed out that if one studies closely the ancient footpaths on almost any parish map one can hardly fail to notice the continuity that exists between the places of worship.

Another of Bob's favourite walks was down Aspley Lane where the drainage was always a problem due to the soil being marl or calcius clay. Aspley Lane winds down from the comparative heights of Strelley village and its ditches on both sides of the thoroughfare held much flowing water, particularly during a rainy summer or autumn. One would imagine this almost constant overflow to have entered the River Leen somewhere near to Bobbers Mill.

The few farmsteads scattered thereabouts were damp and the lane surfaces often resembled a shallow stream. Such consistent winter floodings however, provided pastures of lush grass throughout the summer and dairy cattle seemed to be grazing every second or third field either side of Aspley Lane, while field upon field of potatoes advertised the fact that this was the main, and most successful, crop to thrive in these types of soil.

Pages 10 and 11 of the *Estate Publications Redbook of Nottingham* illustrate the change that has taken place over the past sixty or seventy years. In Section C2, Broxtowe Lane meets with Bells Lane in more or less the same place as it did when both were crossed by footpaths and stiles leading to and from the fields known as Ten Lands. Broxtowe Wood is still featured on the map, although this area is merely a sad remnant of times gone by and so far as I am concerned is best left unexplored-. Eltham Drive roughly covers the length of footpath used by Bob and his friends on their circular walks to and from Basford.

Bob has recently confirmed that the section of the Bells Lane estate known as Amesbury Circus and the circular playing field within, covered a portion of the Ten Lands countryside. Had it been in existence today, the footpath would have swung north and continued through what are now the council house gardens then crossed the loop of Cedarland Crescent and terminated on the edge of the Eastwood By-pass.

Without Bob's assistance however, it would have been difficult to imagine any particular aspects of a landscape, that was perhaps not spectacular, but sent many a local lad a-wandering and unwittingly gathering scenes that would remain within the galleries of his mind for the rest of his life.

A hedge-layering competition: another aspect of heritage and countryside conservation

Camping Out in Lambley Dumbles

Len, whom I've known for thirty-six years, was born in Arnold. He has five brothers and four sisters. A closely knit family, they derived enjoyment from one another's company but became gradually divided when they were about ten or eleven years of age for the girls preferred to stay close to the house and help their mother with her variable chores while the boys spent long hours wandering the streets and, during the school holidays, came home only at mealtimes and dusk.

When each winter came to an end and the evenings began to lengthen, Len and his brothers could hardly wait for the Easter weekend to come around for it was then that they set off for their favourite camping ground in Lambley Dumbles. If an early Easter was scheduled their father would quickly point out that there was still a likelihood of frost chilling and hardening the ground. But, as was the experience of many fathers, his words fell upon deaf ears although Len admits that on several occasions he awoke and, as his father had predicted, it was unbelievably warm inside the tent but outside, the tent covering, its support poles and all the surrounding vegetation were blanketed with hoar frost.

The preparations for these camping forays re-awakened an awareness for adventure, freedom and excitement. And again these three essential ingredients for a happy boyhood permeate within the contours of Len's expressive face, whenever he vividly recalls them.

"For the basic covering of our tent we used the large Tate and Lyle sugar bags which we begged from the grocer at the corner shop or the manager of the local Co-op.

When she had taught us how to sew all the bags together, our mother took a backseat but kept an eye on those of us who had still to master the art of picking three or four loose fibres from one corner and joining them together with the needle and cotton. She often let us use her bodkin so that we could do the job properly.

Once we had the covering for our tent, we gathered up chestnut palings that had been cut to equal lengths and split down the middle so that one had become two. Then, with string we would fasten these together to form the tent's main frame.

The finished product was a tent covering stamped with Tate and Lyle trademarks and standing about five feet high, four feet wide and seven feet long. It was the pride of our young lives and we folded it up carefully when we were going to carry it and unfolded it with equal care when we had reached our little camping ground close to the streams and hawthorn thickets in Lambley Dumbles.

These are a series of small deep valleys where the ground was warm in the summer but the frost lingered long in the winter. To transport all our gear there, we put one lad in the front and he was holding one end of a tent pole while his brother held the other end. Other less fortunate brothers carried the sewn-together 'tent' between them, while the smaller boys and girls carried rucksacks tightly packed with food, blankets, candles and the odd box of matches. We felt like a party of big game hunters out on the African veldt.

Our route was by way of Gedling Lane, which was all fields and farms for as far as you could see to the plateau top road of Mapperley Plains. After walking along here for some way we reached Spring Lane and a stile in the hedge. We had to help one another over with all the equipment, then we walked over seven big fields until we came to those deeply sheltered valleys of our little paradise. Our tent pegs incidentally, were fashioned from twigs and sticks which we cut from the tree branches, usually where there was a 'Y' fork caused by two stems branching from the main stem.

Once the tent was up, we'd unpack the provisions that our mother had prepared for us. There were little tins of pineapple chunks that cost four pence halfpenny each and several tins of Fussels condensed milk. Everything else seemed to be bread and butter sandwiches. She also gave us equal mashings of tea, plates, cups, knives, forks, spoons and billy cans in which we used to boil water on the kindling fires.

We were always collecting kindling but thankfully, the thickets and hedgerows seemed to be choked with it. Once we had the billy can on the fire, we'd drop a little stick onto the water surface and, when it sank, we knew that the water was hot enough for making tea.

We filled the billy cans with the water from the brook. My goodness it was so pure and crystalline you could drink it and dip your face into the deeper pools. It was marvellous.

If clouds seemed to be massing overhead before we snuggled between the blankets inside our tent at dusk, we'd dig a ditch around the structure so that the rainwater drained into it. One thing we did learn though was that our tent wasn't waterproof; not by a long chalk. If it rained heavily, we sometimes had to start packing up because the water would come sluicing straight through the sacking fibres. But we'd never abandon our tent even though it was twice as heavy to carry home, due to it being soaking wet.

There were also mornings – wonderful clear, sunlit mornings when we were awakened by seemingly every cuckoo in the district calling from the trees and thickets and the scents of 'May' blossom would come wafting in on the breeze even before you'd lifted your head from the pillow.

Not that we spent a lot of time listening to the birds singing, lovely though it was. No, sometimes we were naughty little lads in that we'd watch the blackbirds and song thrushes then mark the spot at which the various pairs entered the thicket. About two days later we'd go in and take the eggs. But not all of them I should add, because it became our policy to leave one egg in each.

We took the eggs from the nests of blackbirds, song thrushes, dunnocks and woodpigeons – which lay only two for each clutch anyway. We carried them all in our caps, then we greased one of the billy cans lightly with a knob of lard that our mother had remembered to pack for us, cracked each of the eggs, opened them into the pan and in a matter of minutes had a bird's egg fry up.

Sometimes we'd find a moorhen's nest when exploring the streamsides. Their eggs soon filled the billy can because they're not that smaller than those of a domestic hen. I've still got my billy cans stored in the loft of my house at Wollaton where I've lived for the last thirty-four years and I remember the crockery we used to pack because quite a lot of it our mother managed to get by saving so many coupons at a time then sending off to the local newspaper that was advertising the bargain and promoting each household with the prospect of gaining a stock of handsome plates, cups and saucers at the same time.

Our mother used to send for a china cup and saucer for every pack of coupons she managed to collect. At one time, she sent for a full china tea service. Mind you, with two adults and ten children sitting at the table we needed it! And china was remarkably cheap in those days. In fact, everybody seemed to own a china tea service and a stack of other crockery besides.''

Houghton's Farm and New Farm Wood

A local itinerant still spends most of his day wandering the areas that he knew as a boy. These are Bulwell and Nuthall. Of the latter place he says, ''I used to spend a lot of my time out in the fields around Hempshill Hall. The big farm there was owned by the Houghtons (pronounced *Hooton* in Nottinghamshire) and the family, such as it was, comprised of two brothers and a sister. None of them got married. One of the brothers had only one arm. He may have lost the other in the war, I don't know because they were not the kind of people who mixed readily with other folk so you never really found out very much simply because so little was known about them.

But I'd keep close to the hedgerows when I went onto their fields in the summer afternoons. Not because I was afraid of being seen by the Houghtons but because I wanted to watch the barn owls. There was a pair nested at the farm right from the Thirties through until the Fifties and perhaps after that. Sometimes you'd see them in broad daylight. The parent birds mostly hovering along the ditches like great white moths, then pouncing on a mouse or vole and flying back to the barn loft with it clutched in the talons.

When I managed to get close to the outbuildings I could hear the young owls hissing and snorting. Then, at sunset, the parents would be out again and as they flew, the sunlight seemed to gild their backs and the edges of the wings. It was a lovely sight and one that I don't think I'll ever forget.

One of my favourite woods though has been split now by the MI Motorway. That's New Farm Wood. The oaks there are quite magnificent and in the summer, the bracken fronds are high as your elbow.

A car was dumped there in the 1950s and nobody bothered to tow it away, so it's still where it was abandoned. Just a rusted skeleton almost hidden by bracken and briars. But I could take you straight to it if you wanted to go.''

Backaching Work

An eighty-one-year-old lady born at Radcliffe-on-Trent remembered running chores to the grocers and post office for her mother, then added.

''We young children would all meet up and stand talking in shop doorways or on street corners. Then we'd see some inmates of the Radcliffe Asylum being escorted down the main street by their wardens and nurses and we used to shout after the poor devils, especially a really well-dressed lady who always wore a lovely wide-brimmed hat.

We got to know somehow that her name was Polly and as she came by clutching the two or three pennies she'd been given to buy something with, we'd all begin shouting:

It's Polly, Polly
Polly, Polly, Polly
Polly, Polly, Polly
From the Asylum

And do you know, we young girls were just as cruel as the lads. We'd heckle and follow them down the street, chanting and shouting about the poor beggars just to let everybody know where they'd come from. But we never got close because Polly had a big umbrella that she used to lift threateningly in our direction to let us know she'd mean business if ever she got hold of us.

Mind you, we youngsters had to work as well you know and when we weren't helping our mothers around the big, black leaded kitchen range we'd be out in the fields during the school holidays picking up stones for the farmers.

God, it was backaching work stone picking. There'd be a lot of us, you know, but we weren't allowed to talk much among ourselves. Then, when the stone picking days were over, we reassembled and walked the fields and furrows with a bag of cabbage seeds strung over our shoulders and we had to drop one seed in each of the holes the farm labourers had dug. It wasn't quite as bad as stone picking, but it was hard work for all that and at the end of the week we were each paid the sum of one shilling and sixpence. Mind you, that was a tidy sum of money to us working class folk in those days.''

Postman and Stockman

Earning extra money was very much on the minds of most working class folk during the times of which I write and the postman was no exception. Like most countrymen he could turn his hand to tasks other than sorting and delivering mail.

Some postmen were skilled at hedging and ditching. Others planted seeds or picked stones from land scheduled for ploughing. One I knew specialised in making, selling or renting out scarecrows. But the majority were adept at milking cows and mucking out cowsheds and because they were so keen the local farmers employed them on a regular part-time basis. This, of course, provided the postman and his family with two settled incomes and, for the man, a pleasant and contrasting way of life.

After sorting and delivering the mail, the postman had breakfast then settled down at home, perhaps dozing for a couple of hours after dinner, before visiting the farm in time for milking which was, and often still is', set for around four in the afternoon.

By the time he has returned home and eaten the evening meal the postman of present times still has an hour or two in which to relax, but before the Herringbone Parlour form of milking was introduced, attending the needs of a large herd of cows took up the rest of his day and he had probably just enough time to acknowledge and play with his children before supper time came around.

Up to a Heron's Nest

''When I was a lad there were four species of owl breeding within a half mile radius of the village. Tawnies begin nesting from the end of February to the beginning of March. They use the same site year after year and our local pair hatched off their annual brood of owlets in a hollow tree. About two fields away was the farm and a pair of barn owls nesting in the barn.

The long eared owls used an old magpie's nest built deep in a hawthorn thicket. They hunted south of the village while over to the west there was a pair of little owls nesting in a pollard willow alongside a winterborne stream.

When we village youths had located these I started chafing about never having seen herons at the nest, so one Saturday I went with my dad to Rolleston Goss at Staythorpe near Southwell.

'Goss' was an old Nottinghamshire term for gorse but, at that time, there were no gorse thickets there. It was all pine trees, with rooks nesting at one end and herons another.

Well, there was no-one about, so I chose the tree I was going to climb and the hen bird at the nest I had chosen surprised me by staying until I was about three feet below the platform of twigs and branches. Only then did she take off, but reluctantly. And do you know when I looked into the hollow, two of the chicks had hatched and the other two were breaking through the shell. They did look strange, those young herons. Long beaks, bulging eyes, bluish fluff and hardly the strength to squat in the nest hollow.

Anyway I climbed down quickly and carefully and that heron was back on the nest before I'd actually reached the ground.

Rolleston, by the way, is the village where soldiers who survived the First World War were given Ex-Servicemen's Agricultural Grants to set themselves up as farmers and, needless to say, quite a number of holdings were established between the two World Wars but whether any of the original families are there today I couldn't say for certain.''

The Tallest Tree in Nottinghamshire

As the author of this book, I'm going to allow myself a singular recollection, in this chapter at least.

The location was situated less than a quarter of a mile from my boyhood home on Chalfont Drive and I have described elsewhere the rough track known as Colliers Fad, that connected Radford Woodhouse with the mining community living in terraced squares at Cinderhill and Basford.

If you remember, I mentioned in the chapters relating to Lionel Baker the 'Humps and Hollows' field which, by the time I was born, had lost its gangs of young colliers to the streets and terraces of adulthood.

Nor by this time was there a hedgerow separating the field from Colliers Pad because according to one white bearded sage, ''all them low branches and thickets had been hacked to pieces, carted off and burnt on Guy Fawkes nights''. But there was still a wide ditch filled with nettles and dog's mercury, as well as sprigs of elder and hawthorn. Skylarks seemed to be singing from dawn until dusk and a few cowslips nestled among the breeze-furled stalks of meadowgrass.

And towering above the field and ditch, like a great mute icon, was an elm tree with a straight, almost unclimable trunk and outflung branches so high they created little by way of a cooling shadow when you were sitting listening to the skylarks on hot summer afternoons. That tree was a landmark.

I saw it from my parents' back bedroom window, dwarfing the red tiled rooftops of the private housing estate on which we lived. I glimpsed it when I turned up the next road, Westholme Gardens, a cul de sac where lived my boyhood friends, Roy, Malcolm and Dave.

I was aware of it when I reached the railway bridge on Western Boulevard and could even pick it out among the clusters of trees and rooftops when I stood on the north facing steps of Wollaton Hall. Only visual ignorance and days of thick fog could obliterate that elm whose distant outline was etched black and a deeper black against a build up of dark metallic thunder clouds.

It emphasised the silence that precedes such storms. It made me aware of the timescale to such an extent that, even as a boy, I used to wonder how many past generations of Nottingham folk had known and marvelled at the grandeur of that tree. Then, over the years, I began to take it for granted. The elm was always there. *Would always be there.*

But on the day after I was demobbed from the Royal Air Force, I received two environmental shocks. First I discovered that my beloved boyhood canal had been drained and filled with topsoil and rubble then, as I neared the house, saw a space in the sky where once the elm had stood.

"Mum, what's happened to the tree? Did it get struck by lightning?" I asked. "No. They've chopped it down. They're going to build on the Humps and Hollows field."

"But the tree could have stayed." "Well obviously they didn't think so. Somebody has decided that it must go."

And so that great elm had felt the bite of the axe and woodsaw. Thirty years later I was talking with a man who was keen to recall his days spent around Cherry Orchard and Radford Woodhouse. "There was a tree alongside Colliers Pad that people used to walk from Nottingham just to see. They called it 'The Tallest Tree in Nottinghamshire' because Aspley and Wollaton weren't within the City boundary by then. They'd take summer picnics to the fields and at first I heard that the tenant farmer at Aspley Hall didn't take kindly to what he called an invasion of his land. But I think he mellowed a bit over the years. I mean – we all do, don't we?''.

In writing now at the age of fifty-three, I can say that I have never yet seen a tree as tall as the elm whose height I couldn't estimate since even as a boy I had never considered it in terms of height. Tourists travel north to see the chained remnants of The Major Oak in Sherwood Forest. But its grandeur lies in the width of its trunk or bole. Perhaps also in its original spread of branches. But never in its height.

Today, I think my elm would have been preserved despite the houses and bungalows surrounding it and, in my opinion, Elm Tree Drive would have been a more fitting name than Redbourne Drive which has since overlaid the original Colliers Pad alongside which this great tree once stood.

FURTHER RECOLLECTIONS

Smallholding Swapshops

From a man born during the First world War, I learned the following:

"When I was a boy, Hucknall's central hub was a tough competitive place. Colliers, farmers, gardeners and market traders all seemed to be competing with one another and, if two people happened to be attempting to sell the same product, there was a war on locally, that there was.

In some cases it was 'dog eat dog'. Quite a few families had converted their allotment gardens into small holdings and they were really self-sufficient, growing almost everything except cannabis, but even that wouldn't have surprised me.

Livestock rustling took place regularly as well. 'Swap shop' was nothing alongside the kind of things that went off there. A man would lock up three pigs one night, come back in the morning and find the pigs gone and six hens in their place.

The message as I read it was: "We've taken your pigs but at least we've left you something to be going on with. That's better than nothing at all, don't you think so, me o'wd duck?"

Listening to The Trains

Syd Clay, who is his boyhood and youth, lived within a mile of the railway at Mansfield and Worksop murmured reflectively; "It's funny but you'd never hear the trains during the day. Well I should think you took it for granted, the noise and the rush and the great columns of grey or cream smoke rising into the frosted sky.

If somebody said there was a goods train coming, well we just ambled up the embankment from the brook and watched in a desultory kind of way. But if they said 'express' we rushed because the train was rushing and that very word generated a kind of excitement that you connected with speed but couldn't explain.

When you were leaning on a bridge looking down at a passenger train, the passengers used to wave to you and we'd wave back. But at night I'd curse the trains because winter dusk or summer heat alike, they'd come whistling and thundering above or between the embankments and sometimes there seemed to be ten or twelve passing in one night. Then in-between, the freighters or express trains, you'd hear the buffers clashing as wagons were linked and unlinked in the sidings. No, I can't remember getting a full night's sleep and Len, me brother was the same. In fact, he used to say it was probably quieter trying to sleep in the middle of the city!

Nottinghamshire Taxidermists

Today many people are familiar with the fact that taxidermy is considered to be a form of art on a par with sculpture or painting. But in Victorian times almost every town and village had its self-taught taxidermist who, to the working class, was simply known as 'the bird stuffer'.

Some of the amateur works were considered poor in quality however, but the interest in preserving natural history specimens reached its pitch around 1915-1940 and the professionalism with it. One gentleman recalls:

Even an ordinary house might have a glass case with stuffed birds in, or a magpie or owl positioned in a glass dome.

People paid keepers to shoot or trap birds for them, but I should say every large country house in England contained some very important collections of stuffed birds and animals which were eventually sold or bequeathed to the City museums when the estate was sold to pay death duties or other such debts.

There were several professional taxidermists in Nottingham at around that time. One of them was a Mr Rose who had a business close to where Sainsburys used to be on Lower Parliament Street. As children, we used to go to Nottingham just to look into his shop window at stag and fallow buck heads mounted on varnished shields. Wigeon and teal drakes or gooseander, long-eared owls, a big boar badger or dog fox were also displayed.

Another well-known local taxidermist was Hibbs of Ollerton. He made his living by setting up some really first class cases of exhibits for both the families and staff living at Welbeck, Thoresby and Rufford.

The Chaworth Musters family at Annesley regularly assigned Hibbs for the task of setting up something for their galleries of stuffed birds, mammals and reptiles which eventually became known as 'the Annesley Park Collection' and was rated as one of the finest in Britain.''

Beside the River Smite

The strongest boyhood memories for Harold, a local Lay preacher, revolved around the rich pastoral valley through which meanders the narrow River Smite.

"I'd go ratting quite frequently with my two brothers along the banks of the Smite. We took the terriers with us and, I expect, made quite a bit of noise because never once did we escape the gaze of the estate game keeper. Even if you sat quietly beside the water, you never heard him walking, but you'd see him alright as soon as you looked toward the coverts or the bridge on which he sometimes stood. He appeared just like an apparition. A slightly-built man who never uttered a word, but just stood and looked at what we were doing and smiled in a somewhat contemplative way. We used to carry on talking among ourselves and as you can imagine, it felt pretty uncomfortable with him looking on. But then we'd glance in his direction and he'd be gone, just as silently as he had appeared. It was all a bit weird really.

In the autumn, oh quite some weeks after the harvest and when the pheasant shooting season was well underway, we'd take sacks to the oak woods and fill them with leaf mould then drag them home between us, so that our dad could dig the mould into the soils of his vegetable plot and front garden border. Two of the loveliest oak woods in the area were known as Fern Covert and Thorntons Holt. An artificial fox earth had been established in each.

Thorntons Holt was quite close to Stragglethorpe. My, it was a splendid little wood. Not much undergrowth, but you could stand quietly on the cushioned carpets of leaf mould and watch all the woodland birds and I used to do this throughout the seasons of the year. I can also remember Stragglethorpe village. It was really a hamlet you know. Just two or three farmworkers' cottages, a keeper's house and a cluster of stables and pig sties. They stood just about where the spoil heaps for Cotgrave Colliery were sited. It's a safe bet that the foundations of almost every holding in Stragglethorpe could be unearthed from beneath the spoil

As for Thorntons Holt – well, that's gone. There's a caravan site there now. But could you really call that progress? I somehow doubt it myself."

Christmas in The Workhouse

Alice was born in the workhouse not far from Bingham.

"1 think the buildings have all been pulled down now. I lived there with my mother – and sister Aimie. I never knew my father. We always seemed to be making wicker baskets, plaiting ropes for cloths or fashioning clothes pegs and when I asked why we had always to be working with our hands, she'd say:

"Got to survive. It's either this or picking stones on the farmer's fields and we're not doing that for a living.

But the Christmases were nice. We made garlands – all the women and girls alike and we'd be wrapping oranges and new pennies and sugar pigs in silver paper then exchanging them for more or less of the same things on Christmas morning.

On Christmas Eve the vicar would call accompanied by the church choir and we'd all sing carols around the Christmas tree. Then on Christmas morning you'd watch mother putting the goose or turkey in the oven because, although we couldn't afford either, the farmers were very kind and they used to bring poultry round to be plucked and drawn a day or so before Christmas, but we never knew for certain whether we'd be given one for the family, although we always were. No one went without.

On Boxing Day, about half past eleven, there was great excitement generated throughout the rooms because first we'd hear the clatter of horse shoes and then, when we went to the windows, there'd be the Hunt in scarlet and black regalia descending on the workhouse and wishing all our mothers 'good morning' as they reined their magnificent horses in front of the building and spent a few minutes talking and enquiring, if we were having a nice Christmas. I was always a bit wary of the horses, but my sister used to go out and stroke their necks and muzzles while me and Henrietta, my friend, used to beg some big meat bones from the cook and these we would give to the hounds; with the Huntmaster's approval of course."

Home Cured Bacon

While talking to a lady who lived alone in a cottage not far from Cotgrave, I happened to mention pig keeping, a subject of which she was once quite familiar since she and her late husband had kept two or three pigs in a stye situated at the far end of the garden.

She then said: "Seventy or eighty years ago, almost every cottage had a stye holding one to four pigs and each autumn, one would be taken up to the village for slaughter. In the early days, two men would come with goading sticks and a bunch of kiddies and drive the pigs along the roads. But by the time I was ten or eleven, I got used to seeing a car and trailer pulling up outside and my dad walking down the path to greet the local butcher and his assistant.

Most of the pigs taken to his yard had their throats cut and when they had been cleaned and bled, whole pigs were hung by the hindquarters on a rail outside the butcher's shop window. At intervals, you'd see a man come out of the shop carrying a pail of water, half of which he poured over each carcass. After being hung in this manner, the cottager's pig was salted on a low cement slab called a 'Binky' then it was jointed and split into hams and bacon. These were eventually returned to the cottager or holder with a message to say that they were ready to be collected and the sides of bacon and hams were hung from the low beams in the cellar, pantry, kitchen and living room, if it was found to be necessary. Occasionally a butcher and his client would negotiate over the carcass of a freshly killed pig, but an exchange of either meat or money took place and none got a bad deal out if it.

Some cottages were fitted with their own 'binkys once they got the art of salting a pig. In fact, the children enjoyed rubbling salt into the skin just as much as the adults, but I can't imagine anyone doing it today although it would do them good to have a try.''

Grannie Simmond's Bridge

The left side of the steep hill leading from Wollaton Village to Trowell Moor, was massed with oaks, sweet chestnuts, sycamores and pines. At the top was Balloon Woods, an extensive area of woodland, bracken, brambles and sand-pits with carpets of bluebells thriving on the shaded slopes.

The narrow road left the walker with the impression that it terminated where two small turnpike cottages stood on either side, but beyond the cottages, a ridge road connected the Erewash Valley villages of Sandiacre and Stapleford to the west with Strelley village and the farms of Broxtowe and Bilborough at its easterly swing.

This ridge road was called Blackbird Lane, but the name-refers not to that member of the thrush family which frequents the woods and hedgerows, but the rooks which fed across the fields in large flocks and nested in the elms of the Wollaton, Trowell and Strelley Halls.

While taking in the turnpike scene, it would not be unreasonable for anyone to have asked how the name of Balloon Woods came about, nor how the two little cottages were similarly named Balloon Houses by almost everyone living on the north-west side of the county. Of the many people with whom I have spoken, few can give a precise answer, but scanty recollections suggest that hydrogen balloons were released and maintained there by a local army unit who used the surrounding fields as a training ground during the First World War. Certainly the turnpike cottages were much older than their wartime name might suggest and the origin of each was no doubt carried within the mind of Grannie Simmonds who had lived in one of them.

Her background and her husband's employment, had long been forgotten, but she was widowed by the time that many of the children, born around the turn of the century, had made their way up to Balloon Woods and carried home bluebells by the armful. A lady, who wishes to remain anonymous, not only provided me with a photograph of Grannie Simmonds, but furnished me with the following lines.

Grannie Simmonds, who lived in a tollgate cottage at Balloon Wood crossroads

"With her long striped dresses, ruffle-necked blouse and black walking stick, Grannie Simmonds considered herself to be the guardian of Balloon Woods.

She was never averse to letting someone use her back garden privy or handing out glasses of water to village folk out walking on a hot summer day. But woe betide them if they were seen picking wild flowers or birdnesting along the lanes.

"Grannie Simmonds lived off the land as best she could. Both gamekeeper and poacher would surreptitiously call on her, carrying a brace of rabbits, woodpigeon or pheasants. But jealously guarded was her recipe for pickling walnuts. Nor would she ever volunteer the whereabouts of the big sweet chestnuts that she used to roast in the hearth. You'd see her out every day nearly. Collecting kindling or filling baskets with berries and mushrooms, but goodness, if she saw you in Balloon Woods, she'd come along the path waving her black stick with her conical black hat making all the younger children think they were being pursued by a witch. She belonged to that generation who carried recipes for almost everything, including curing warts, did Grannie Simmonds, and she was moved by superstitions to do with the weather or the shape of the moon.

Attached to her little cottage, was an orchard filled with apple, pear and plum trees and on warm evenings at the end of the summer, she used to hobble down

Blackbird Lane to where the woods fringed the edge of the canal. Often she'd be carrying a basket or bucket filled with these orchard fruits, but when she was younger she used to stand on the bridge and look at the sunset or listen to the birdsong filtering through the trees.

As she became older and people got used to seeing her about, they'd stop and have a word with her; particularly the bargees and their families who sometimes moored for the night alongside the wooded towpath.

The bridge incidentally was first known as Cliffords Bridge because a family of stockmen carrying that name lived in one of the two cottages standing in the middle of the nearby fields. A gamekeeper lived next door and both families were employed by the landowners who resided at Bramcote Hall. Over the years though the owners of the barges began to call it Grannie Simmonds Bridge, because she was often to be seen there; what used to take place was an exchange between Grannie Simmonds and the bargees of fruits from the orchard and lumps of coal from the bargee's load.

If Grannie Simmonds happened to miss a bargee family, she'd leave a bucket of apples or pears in a little wooden hollow by the buttresses of the bridge and go the next day to collect the bucket of coal that they had left in exchange.

Aye, If there was one old dear who knew how to survive in those days it was Grannie Simmonds, but goodness knows what she'd think if she saw the bridge and the woods – or the remains of them – for they have been badly neglected over the past thirty or forty years. The poor old girl – she'd turn in her grave, that she would.''

The Lure of a Gleaming River

Throughout the last years of her life the late Margaret Shipside lived in a gatehouse belonging to the Flintham Hall estate. Due to her superlative work with sick and injured birds she found that she could count upon the support of a wide circle of friends and also welcomed to her home, people who were keen to learn how to rear and rehabilitate tiny nestlings or young hawks, falcons and owls.

Before moving into the Lodge on the Fosse, as Margaret called her last home, she lived in a spacious, double-fronted house overlooking the River Trent at Gunthorpe. Here, she specialised in receiving and rehabilitating large water birds such as mute swans and Canada geese which she allowed to roam the large orchard at the rear of the house.

Like most people, Margaret was deeply attracted to water and savoured the Trent for its aesthetic values; its shimmer, width and moods created by angles of light and formations of cloud.

To use her own words: "For most of my life I have always answered to the lure of a gleaming river."

Like myself, Margaret never lost this awareness and enjoyed the additional solitude that one can still find by walking the towpath of the Grantham Canal. Some days she would cycle out to the remote villages and hamlets, locate the waterway and explore it alone. At other times she was a passenger in a Wolseley car driven by an ageing aunt who, after parking the vehicle, accompanied Margaret on her rambles.

On one of my many visits to her Gunthorpe home, Margaret showed me photographs and snapshots of stretches of the canal that one would hardly recognise today and hump backed bridges which might still be standing, but are seldom used by anyone other than the stockman tending his herd of Freisian cattle. Some of these snapshots may have been taken by the only love of her life, as she once described a wartime boyfriend to me. They depicted Margaret standing beside various bridges, disused lock-gates and lines of willow thicket that have been long hacked down by some tidy minded lengthman.

Margaret's favourite local landscape however was the long ridge that weaves between Radcliffe on Trent and Shelford. She loved its contours and the winding, escarpment-like bends along which she drove in her grey Wolseley.

"This," she told me one afternoon when I was in the passenger seat beside her, "is called the Malkin Hill. Isn't it splendid?"

On one occasion she mentioned the autumn mist creeping over fields and gradually enveloping the chequerboard landscape below. This observation alone endorsed her perception and delight in the changing seasons.

On midsummer afternoons, Margaret would often drive out alone to The Dukeries and picnic in a woodland glade. Or, if she hadn't the time to travel far, she sometimes chose to picnic in Kneeton Woods which gave her some unrestricted views of her beloved 'gleaming river'.

Many people living in the Lowdham-Gunthorpe area will remember Margaret in her occupational role of school teacher at the old schoolhouse in Gunthorpe village. She was also a regular churchgoer and loved arranging the flowers according to the time of year.

If this gentle lady was with us today I think she would choose among her fondest memories those days spent with the children, whose names she remembered long after they had left school. Of the river, I am sure she would have enthused about the school midsummer holidays when, at some pre-dawn hour, she packed a flask of tea, took a rowing boat from the Gunthorpe boatyard and rowed quietly down to where the water lapped alongside the Shelford coverts. Here she would rest with her oars in the rowlocks and quietly sip her tea, while listening to the river talk of coots and moorhens ferrying through the reedstems. Frequently her patience was further rewarded when a nightingale burst into song from a hidden perch within a few feet of its delighted admirer.

Such moments became deeply etched within Margaret Shipside's unfailing memory and served to enhance her years spent in the Nottinghamshire she so loved.

Notable Farmers

Several of Nottinghamshire's farmers and landowners became keen stock-breeders with Lord Spencer of Wiseton receiving prominence for the quality of his cattle that took many prizes at Smithfield. If today you happen to be walking or driving close to the semi-industrial scene near Clifton Bridge, Lenton, you might try to imagine the fields grazed by a strain of Dairy Shorthorn cattle pioneered by John Wilkinson of Grove Farm, Lenton.

North of the City the fields to the east of Bestwood's Big Wood were owned by the Duke of St Albans whose tenancies – Top House Farm and Bottom House Farm – were managed by John and William Lamin respectively.

When Nottinghamshire hosted the Royal Agricultural Show in 1915 both brothers won prizes for having maintained the best arable farms throughout the East Midlands. Further accolades occurred during wartime when they were mentioned in respect of how admirably farm produce could be harvested from difficult and sandy land. The Lamin brothers also grazed a herd of Dairy Shorthorn cattle and after the war received recognition for being the first Nottinghamshire farmers to have grown sugar beet.

A GARDENER'S LIFE

Gardening and estate maintenance were full-time occupations that ensured a man could earn a steady wage and either live in a tied cottage or pay rent for an equally compact dwelling, situated in the village or within close proximity of the country estate.

The average estate employed several gardeners and estate workers according to the acreage of ground that needed to be maintained. For example, a five-hundred-acre estate would provide enough work for twenty-two men and a larger area, thirty to thirty-five men. Some gardeners were employed in both the kitchen gardens and the ornamental grounds while others, with perhaps a skill or speciality for nurturing certain types of shrubs and plants, might remain in one place.

During the autumn, the apprentice estate workers and keepers were to be seen along the lime avenues, sweeping the leaves into piles which were then heaped onto the back of a four-sided cart and used as leaf mould, along with mounds of horse manure which was daily raked from the stables and stored in a similar manner.

Boys of fourteen or fifteen who had just left school were put on the pay-roll, their first tasks being to pick up litter, twigs and tree branches that might have come down during an overnight gale. Any gaps that appeared in the fences or tree boughs that came crashing to the ground were reported to the estate steward or the joiner and woodsman, if the boy happened to meet them before they had seen the damage.

The kitchen garden walls were built eight to ten feet high and of local, red brick. Many were designed so that a series of inner walls served as windbreaks and to divide off the various plots of land.

Here the head gardener spent much of his time instructing the apprentices how to plant out everything from lettuce seedlings to lupins, store daffodil and tulip bulbs and keep the tools of the trade clean and oiled and ready for immediate use the following day.

He checked the beds of strawberries and gooseberries, the rows of black and red currants and quietly rebuked the understudy to the foreman if he noticed weeds collecting in the herb garden. He also ensured that the piles of leaf mould and horse manure looked tidy, should anyone from the Hall have decided to wander down for a look around or have collected for themselves, a few sprigs of mint and rosemary.

Most of the family's fruit and vegetables were grown in the gardens: pumpkins, potatoes, beans, peas, carrots, asparagus, artichokes, turnips and loganberries. Apples, pears, plums and damson trees flourished and apricots, peaches and nectarines were propagated and harvested from the myriads of branches strung out along one of the inner walls.

Many such walls had been designed with the propagation of tropical fruits specifically in mind. Subsequently they were hollow and had at one end, several small bothies or living quarters, each of which was installed with an oven and fire range, small clothes line for drying out wet garments, sink and single bed.

Here a selection of the gardening staff took it in turns to stay overnight; their overall task being to keep the fires that were lit within the hollowed wall alight and blazing, so that the bricks were constantly warmed and the peaches and apricot branches remained free from frost or snow that would have otherwise killed them off.

The bothie workers, as they were known, sometimes spent three to four nights a week tending the wall fires in the kitchen gardens and were usually served meals by the staff living at the nearest gate lodge. Many gate lodge families also took in their washing.

Besides the wall fires, these men had also to check and inspect the tropical fruits growing in the 'orangery' where not only oranges but bananas and eucalyptus plants were also encouraged to thrive.

The centre piece for most ornamental gardens was the conservatory designed with cast iron framework and many panes of glass which created a humid atmosphere, thus ensuring that ferns, palms, bamboo, camellias and orchids were given the right conditions. The conservatory was visited by several members of staff, including the head gardener, throughout each working day.

In the season, geraniums were planted in all the varying shaped urns; clematis and other climbing plants were positioned so that the flowering vines caught the stroller's eye when he, or she, was passing through a doorway. Even the entrance to the potting shed garden was partially screened by bowers of honeysuckle, clematis or cotoneaster.

In some ornamental gardens at least one bothie had been built next to the potting sheds and if a foreman gardener chose not to live there, then he at least spent a few nights in the bothie, particularly if he was required to hose the flower beds after dark during a spell of warm, dry weather.

Interior of The Orangery, Wollaton Park. (Photograph: F.Parkes)

The lawn of almost every country house garden was positioned alongside the gravel walks and close to the terraces and french windows. Resembling green velvet carpets, the lawns were mown at least once a week during the summer months. This lengthy operation was usually scheduled to take place on a Thursday or Friday, so that the family and their guests could enjoy uninterrupted views of the gardens and stroll the lawns throughout each weekend.

The grass cutting machine, although called simply 'the mower', was a horse-drawn contraption which mowed a yard's width and had razor-sharp cutter blades. The professional name for this necessary piece of equipment was called 'The Greens Machine' since it had been designed by someone of that name.

Attached to the front was a box which collected all the cut grass and any tufts that were missed were trimmed down by a second set of blades which were positioned so that the cut grass blades were immediately heaped into the box at the rear.

When both mowing boxes were full, the grass was either dumped into the hollow of a tree or taken by wheelbarrow to a piece of spare land alongside the courtyard filter beds.

There were two men working The Greens Machine; one guiding the machine at the rear, the other gently leading a blinkered estate horse by the bridle, along and across each section of lawn as it needed to be mown.

Accompanying the two men were one or more boys who, in the singular, was known as 'the side man'. His, or their, job was to walk in front of the horse pulling The Greens Machine and pick up any twigs or stones that may have been scattered upon the turf. Before mowing commenced, the horse's feet were each fitted into a baggy type of boot which was strapped around the hocks. To put such a boot onto the horse's foot, the man had only to gently tap one leg and it would lift back the hoof in readiness for strapping

All four feet were booted in this manner to prevent the prints of horse shoes becoming engraved upon the turf.

Another of the side men's duties was to have a can or bucket of water standing in a nearby patch of shrubbery for, if the horse urinated on the turf, water would have to be thrown upon the spot otherwise large brown patches would appear because the urine had not scaled quickly into the ground.

Towards the end of a working day, the men would sweep the gravel walls with besoms, clean and oil their tools and utensils; then cart all the cuttings and debris in wheelbarrows to the rubbish heap.

Goldfish in the ornamental ponds were fed in the last few minutes, then in the works yard grain was scattered for the fantailed pigeons and peacocks, for most gardeners preferred to see peafowl around the outbuildings yard rather than the ornamental gardens because these fine ornamental birds also pecked the heads and petals from flowers in full bloom.

All of the afore-mentioned tasks and routines were undertaken by a retinue of gardening staff who were supervised by a foreman and he, in turn, was responsible to the head gardener.

In the same way that other responsible servants and employees kept in touch with the occupational requests of the titled family living at the Hall, so the head gardener made his presence known, especially during the summer months, when at eleven thirty on each Saturday morning he and his foreman carried buckets filled with freshly cut flowers, up to the house and these they would give to the butler, who in turn passed them to a maid whose job it was to arrange them in the vases and keep them watered throughout the weekend.

One retired head gardener who had been employed for forty years on an estate in north west Nottinghamshire, added: "Oh aye, and usually if his Lordship or Ladyship happened to have been around when you were handing the flowers to the butler, they'd invite you into their sitting room where we were given a glass of sherry or port; or even whisky if we were lucky.

Yet the story was different if we were working outside and the family were driven up to the front door in their chauffeur driven Rolls Royce or Daimler. For if they happened to see a gardener trimming the edges of the lawns or sweeping the gravelled forecourt, they wouldn't bother ringing the bell and stand waiting for the butler or valet to open the door, but expect instead the gardener to come sprinting across and ring the bell for them.

There was one chap, Harry Hughes, who detested having to do that, but if the task happened to have fallen upon his shoulders, he used to come stalking into the workshed, light up a cigarette and begin his grumbling saying; "They never so much as intend to turn a brass door knob these people. God knows what would happen if they actually had to do a day's physical work to get some money rolling in like we do."

The few remaining souls who were employed at Wollaton Hall and Park in Victorian/Edwdwardian times remember with affection the head gardener whom they were always willing to serve, due to the feeling of team spirit he so admirably promoted amongst them.

Frederick William Parkes was a Yorkshire man, born into the village community of Wykeham, seven miles south of Scarborough. Even as a boy, he showed a keen interest in plants and flowers and on leaving school acquired the first threads of horticultural knowledge while employed in a large propagation complex in Scotland, close to Loch Long.

Frederick William Parkes, Superintendent of Wollaton Park

After gaining an early reputation for rearing orchids, he travelled south to spend the next four years working on the Royal estate at Sandringham, Norfolk. He was at first reluctant to work under the strict eye of the Royal head gardener, but after a few months he settled down and continued to quench his thirst for horticultural knowledge.

During a particularly cold and frosty winter, he discovered that King Edward and Queen Alexandra shared a passion for ice skating on the surface of the frozen lakes with their friends and relatives.

Frederick was at Sandringham when George V married Queen Mary, but shortly after the wedding he found a gardener's position at Stoneleigh Abbey Warwickshire, where he met and married the daughter of a lady who had been employed as housemaid to the Duke of Connaught at his country estate house in the centre of Bagshot Park, Surrey.

Both mother and daughter were employed as maids at Stoneleigh when Fred arrived there. After the wedding, the couple moved to north Nottinghamshire having both served positions at a small country house near Retford.

Here, they began to collect furniture and get a home together until Frederick saw an advertisement in a horticultural weekly, saying that a head gardener was required on Lord Middleton's eight hundred acre estate at Wollaton.

Frederick applied and secured this position which provided the anchorage he had been seeking. Realising that he had got a good position on a fine estate situated perhaps less than three miles from the city centre, he remained at Wollaton until the day he retired.

The young couple moved into the head gardener's cottage in 1903. The cottage was screened from the beautifully landscaped acres of Wollaton Park by a high wall and remains so to this day. It also backed onto the estate's home farm and was close to the lodge and the bothie of the kitchen gardens, thus a small community spirit was nurtured around that particular corner of Wollaton Park, as undoubtedly it was on other country estates where people lived and worked beside one another.

Wilfred Widdowson, who was employed on the Wollaton Park estate for fifty-five years says of Frederick Parkes: 'He was such a kindly man that everyone called him 'Father'. He loved flowers, shrubs, dogs, photography and people. He also knew that because he was liked and well respected, he could get the best work out of his men.

The working day in those times began at six in the morning until five in the afternoon, summer and winter alike. At eight though, everyone stopped for breakfast which was eaten close to wherever we were working. Mind you, if 'Father' Parkes was walking in the direction where he knew a gang of men to be working, he used to whistle to let them know he was coming. But he was no fool. He knew the whereabouts of every man and if he happened to run out of cigarettes, he'd send one of the lads around to all the men, then they'd write down what they wanted on a notepad and then when it was returned to him, 'Father' used to ride his bicycle to the shop in Wollaton Village and collect everyone's order.

Freda Parkes outside the Head Gardener's cottage, Wollaton Park. (Photograph: F.Parkes)

Why, I have seen the time when a man had smoked his last cigarette and Father had given him 'another to be going on' with until he got back from the shop. He was a wonderful man and because he was such a good friend, we gave every ounce of sweat for any job he asked us to do.''

WIlfred began his long term of employment at Wollaton Hall and Park in January 1916, for a wage of six shillings a week. Employed in the kitchen gardens he soon familiarised himself with the Orangery, a semi-circular building, fronted by a paved path bordered with flower beds. Ornamental trees were positioned into every nook and cranny, including eucalyptus trees, which 'Father' Parkes inspected daily.

Upon entering the Orangery, one had to descend two or three steps and walk a flagstoned path beneath which a series of pipes were laced together so that the building was kept heated by the coal burning consistently from a large boiler.

The park's coal was delivered from Wollaton Pit and cost sixpence a ton. Large lumps were used to keep the boiler and Orangery heated by day, whereas at night the boiler was covered with slack and the waste raked out first thing the following morning.

Kitchen garden and propagation staff at Wollaton Park, c.1920. Note that foremen wore bowlers and the workmen sported caps. (Photograph: F.Parkes)

In the sheds and bothies of the kitchen gardens were stacks of plant pots, potato sacks and cases used for packing apricots and peaches.

Pear trees flanked many of the paths and Wilfred, while talking to me in his seventy-ninth year, stated emphatically that most of the springtime crocuses which flourished within the walled confines of Wollaton Hall's kitchen gardens, had been flourishing there for the past forty-five years.

Wilfred also remembers the yew trees in both the park and around 'Father' Parkes' cottage being tapered to a point and as soon as they began to thicken, two men were hastily assigned to trim them back into the desired shape.

White chrysanthemums were grown in the greenhouses and later in the year, pyracantha branches were cut by 'Father' who took them up to the village church where they were used to decorate the font.

During the hot weather 'Father' used to send Wilfred round to the home farm with a bucket to collect a gallon of milk. When he returned, he was then told to put a syringe pipe into the bucket and spray the milk onto the glass panes of each greenhouse, so that the plants would receive some noticeable degree of shade.

At breaktime, Wilfred and other youngsters paid another visit to the home farm dairy. Here they bought milk for one penny a cup, then walked back with it to the bothies, where the men were assembled for coffee.

During the mid-winter snowfalls, the gardeners joined the estate workers with spades and helped them clear the formal drives of snow before putting salt and gravel down.

In 1928, Wilfred was temporarily assigned to a gang of estate workers who were tidying the brashings around the sides of the lake.

"Do you know, the ice was so thick that we piled all the brashings onto it, lit the fire, then boiled the kettle that we carried with us so that we could drink a mug or two of hot tea," he told me.

While recalling those dark winter days, Wilfred mentioned the low, golden glow of gas lights emitting from the outbuildings and the windows of Wollaton Hall. Gas lamps were fixed to the chandeliers in the main rooms of the Hall and two gas lamps were lit and positioned, one each side of the steps leading up to the formal entrance. A huge gas main led up to the Hall buried below ground of course and all the stoves were worked by gas.

In and around the outbuildings, the staff were allowed to use as much coal as they required for their living quarters' fires. By that I mean that they didn't have to pay for it. Consequently, there was a constant trail of wheelbarrows or wooden trolleys being trundled to and from the coal bunkers that were situated close to the doorway of the servants' hall.

Wilfred's grandfather was also employed at Wollaton and it was he who took Wilf aside one day when they were harvesting potatoes and explained that when each potato was firm, a small piece should be cut from the base to prevent it going to seed.

Wilfred also learned that potato seeds were planted with handfuls of soot sprinkled out and around them so that with a bag of seeds and several sacks of soot either side of you it became a 'right mucky' job did planting potatoes.''

Always keen to learn something new, Wilfred discovered that the camellias flowered in March and that their pollination was aided by Fred Meates, or one of his workmates, entering the camelia house about four every afternoon and dusting the flowers with a rabbit's foot strapped to the end of a bamboo cane. ''Yes, it was a totally different world than the one we know today. There were no proper qualifications. It was all done by one man passing on his experiences to another and I swear our flowers were just as bright and our home-grown fruit just as juicy, although I must admit it was damned hard work, but enjoyable nonetheless.''

We return now to the gardener's cottage and Frederick's daughter Freda, who remembers taking her first steps, ''in a fantastic house which was a sheer delight to be living in.''

In common with the theme of most country estate tied cottages, the kitchen dominated much of the household scene. After entering by the front door, the visitor would have found the sitting room on one side and the dining room on the other. The kitchen was directly ahead and the mantelpiece invited a second glance as one walked through the door. Freda was understandably fond of this kitchen which she remembers being: ''A lovely old place furnished by way of a dressing table, long work-table, smaller table and quite a number of chairs. But the pride of our room was the lovely blue Dresden dinner service that we always had on display.

There were baskets of vegetables just about everywhere and braces of pheasants, woodpigeon and rabbits that the keeper had given to us, dangling from the low beams and rafters.

Mind you, we also had to make room along the beams for the sides of bacon that used to dangle over the table, but for smaller items there was plenty of cupboard space for storing sugars, flour, tea, coffee and all kinds of little herbs and condiments.

We had so many kitchen utensils that each big ladle or colander was hung from a nail hammered into the wall. There were three walls filled with kitchen utensils Well it *was* 'Mother's workshop' after all.''

The fireplace was made up of a hob with a hot water boiler on one side and stove on the other. The cellars by contrast were deep, shaded and cool. Freda and her sister Violet had to negotiate a flight of steep steps on the descent.

Though it was always kept immaculate, the walled garden became Freda and Violet's playground with perhaps the most unsightly object being a swing roped to the branches of a damson tree rising from a border over looking the lawn.

To the rear of the house, a small gate in the wall opened out into the kitchen gardens and here the sisters, with their friend Gwen Harden, would walk past all the busy workmen and gardeners to the Orangery, which they regarded as an outsize doll's house.

"The Orangery was a lovely place. Dry and airy. Filled with bowers of eucalyptus, orange and fig trees, grapevines and occasionally bananas." said Freda.

Awed by the myriad of various shaped leaves, the girls wandered the adjacent gravel paths and saw the walls clustered with peaches, apricots and nectarines. When they were very young, they were given to eat two such fruits each day. But if he learned that Lord and Lady Middleton were due to pay a visit, 'Father' Parkes, in his kindly manner, declared the Orangery out of bounds for the girls and added that they were not to be seen eating any of the fruit.

The Orangery paths would then be tidied and swept by a gardener whose workmates would be similarly sweeping the surrounding paths and drives and clearing any piled debris aside.

Occasionally Lady Middleton rode over to the Head gardener's cottage on her white pony and, after speaking for a while with their mother, she would take the girls aside and teach them deportment by balancing books upon their heads. Both girls were also taught how to curtsey correctly. But Freda was, at her own admission 'something of a tomboy' who loved to climb trees to look for birds' nests and watch the red squirrels crossing the lawns and running the gauntlet of the tree branches situated quite close to the house.

One night in early summer, Freda and Violet were awakened by their parents and told to be very quiet as they left the darkened cottage and crossed Goodes Field to Gorsebed Wood. Here they entered the glades and stood listening to the cock nightingales proclaiming the whereabouts of their territorial boundaries.

"And that has since proven to be an unforgettable experience," Freda added.

Occasionally when she was sent out to the shed to fill the buckets with coal for the cottage fires, she heard the huge Friesian bull snorting and stamping in its stable, for the farm stables were adjacent to the cottage outbuildings.

"Yes, you went through another little gate in the wall and found yourself surrounded by free range hens and perhaps the cows waiting to be milked." smiled Freda before adding that she was forever climbing the ladders in the barns and going up to play in the hay lofts.

"I should think I've had the happiest childhood one could ever imagine," said the white haired lady, smiling to herself as she made coffee for us both in the house that she shares with her daughter and is situated within twenty minutes' walk of the cottage where she was born.

An old cottage in Wollaton Road, Nottingham; a typical dwelling for many of those who worked on the grand estates of the area. (F. Parkes)

THE HOUSE BY SKINNER'S LOCK

Situated beside the towpath of the Grantham Canal about four miles from the River Trent, the white house which stands a few yards from Lock No 4 has been the home of a succession of lock keepers and canal lengthmen for a surprising number of years.

The particulars of exactly when the house was built are probably stored in a filing cabinet maintained by the administrative staff of the British Waterways Board who still own the property. The name Skinner's Lock House however gives one the impression that a family of that name was living there at the end of the last century. Eventually it became known as Mrs Skinner's Lock House which suggests, to me at least, that the lady lived alone there after her husband had died.

She most probably continued opening and closing the lock gates in accordance with the demands of the canal traffic and if she had been left a widow then Mrs Skinner would have received the sympathy of all the bargees and their families, for they were basically warm-hearted people, even if they did carry the reputation for being quick-tempered and verbally uncouth among themselves.

The Skinners tenancy ceased about 1902 and the lockhouse was taken over by the Waltons, a Cotgrave family. Like his father and grandfather Mr Walton was a keen shooting man, but shot only for the pot. However game such as rabbits, hares, pheasants and partridge was abundant and during the nesting season not only were the eggs of game-birds collected for breakfast by the knowing countryman but also those of the moorhens and corncrakes that attempted to breed around the reedy pools and dykes.

The lock keeper's family were also allowed free fishing along the stretch of bank extending from the lock gate to the end of the garden. Perch, roach and tench were caught and, in the season, the occasional pike. Vegetables were grown in the garden or bought from the local farmers and market gardeners. In the lockhouse garden today stands a grafted Bramley apple tree that still nurtures a healthy crop of fruit. This was grafted onto an existing tree by Mr

Walton, who brought the graft home from Cotgrave by fastening it across his bicycle. In the autumn the family picked mushrooms and horse chestnuts. Garden fruits and blackberries and raspberries, the wild fruits of the hedgerow, were also gathered and bottled and stored in readiness for each coming winter.

Winter along the Grantham Canal

The bargees transported coal to the Duke of Rutland's estate in the Vale of Belvoir and it would seem that the barges were moored briefly alongside the lock house before they were guided into the pound between the two lock gates. Here, on the canal bank, the lock keeper or a member of the family were given some quite large lumps of coal. Over the years, one or two lumps were accidentally dropped into the water and when the canal was dragged in fairly recent times quite a stock of coal lumps was recovered from the canal bed.

Besides coal, the bargees also transported sewage and one can immediately sympathise with the lock keeper or canal lengthman, when barges loaded with the stuff were steadied before the lock gates were reached and the water levels adjusted so that the bargees could continue their journey. The duties of the lock keeper are self-explanatory but those of the lengthman were more varied. Each man was responsible for keeping his allocated stretch of the canal free from encroaching vegetation, and the banks, towpath and bordering hedgerows in good repair.

The waterway had also to be checked for leaks which, if they occurred, had to be quickly puddled! This was achieved by first reporting the leak to the foreman, who in turn negotiated for the clay boat to be brought along the canal to the leakage point. Once the craft was moored, the lengthman and the clay boat's crew would sink poles gently into the canal bed and when the source of the leak was discovered they waded into the depths and poured clay into the cracks. The men then stamped the clay in with the heels of their wading boots.

While doing this, the canal workers often stood with their backs to the clayboat, held onto the sides and stamped rhythmically until the foreman ascertained that the crack had been filled to his satisfaction. As the canal spanned a distance of thirty-three miles between Nottingham and Grantham, ten lengthmen were employed. Each was given 'three miles and a bit' of the canal to manage.

Along certain sections of the canal towpath small wooden huts were erected. These were designed to hold the lengthmen's tools such as scythes, dragnets, bill hooks, and in later years, grass cutting machinery. A grindstone fastened to a supporting frame was often place nearby.

At the end of the summer the long grass growing beside the hedgerows was scythed and quantities given to the bargees as hay for their horses. However, under the foreman's watchful eye, the main crop of cut grass was raked up, piled beside the water, collected by two men guiding a horse and cart, then transported to the yards of the local farmers and landowners who had previously negotiated with the waterways company and accepted their price for an extra hay crop. This was stored in readiness to feed their cattle and horses in the lean months of winter.

When they couldn't work because of a heavy snowfall or unusually inclement weather several canal lengthmen would meet at their tool cabins where they cajoled while playing cards and dominoes. But no cabin was forgotten and the canal foreman visited each on his bicycle in turn and decided when the men should return to their duties.

When the Waltons needed a brace of pheasants or partridge for the pot they had only to walk down the road to the plot of land on which the Stragglethorpe Nurseries are now based. Here in a cottage built beside three pine trees that are standing to this day lived Mr Coleman one of the gamekeepers employed by the Earl Manvers estate. While it was acceptable for the lock keepers to shoot some rabbits and hares for the pot, game-birds were reared for the shooting parties that set off from Holme Pierrepont Hall and the gamekeepers were held responsible for providing a good crop of birds. Therefore, if a family required a brace they would have needed the gamekeeper's approval and an extra shilling or two with which to buy them.

Sport was also provided for the hunting fraternity. Across the canal and over the field directly opposite the lock keeper's house stands Cotgrave Place. This was the home of the James family who employed a sizeable staff both at the Hall and in the grounds. Most members of the family were particularly interested in field sports. Due to the high regard the titled folk held for the landowner who bred foxes on his land specifically with the hunt in mind-it became fashionable for the estate management team to maintain coverts which were intended to provide harbour for a number of foxes throughout the daylight hours.

Once these were established the vixens were induced to breed in artificial earths which were dug out and lined with bricks in the same way as a drain, but with two exits. A circular breeding chamber was constructed at the end in which each vixen reared her annual litter of cubs.

The canal lengthmen who were employed around Skinner's Lock were eventually informed that if work needed doing along the banks of the Polser Brook it was expected to be undertaken as quickly and quietly as possible for artificial fox earths had also been constructed in the hedgebanks between the brook and the estate steward's house.

The four families of farmworkers who lived at Shepherds Cottages (now Shepherds Restaurant) were also informed and asked to keep away from the coverts at all times. In fact the entire area was regarded to have been out of bounds to everyone except the gamekeeper and his assistant. One young man who was employed as a hedger and general handyman on the Earl Manvers estate was Wilfred Bemrose who eventually married his childhood sweetheart Dolly and applied for the position of canal lengthman when Mr Walton retired after having lived at the lock house for thirty-seven years. Both Wilfred and Dolly were delighted when he was offered the position and moved in almost as soon as the house was vacated.

The couple had known each other almost from the day they could walk. Dolly was the youngest child of a family of fourteen. In the days that she best recalled, her father delivered coal on a horse-drawn dray to houses in Cotgrave and Radcliffe-on-Trent as well as the surrounding farms and keepers' cottages.

Sometimes one or two of the children were allowed to ride with their father on the dray and Dolly chuckled quietly when she described herself as having a mass of gingery red curly hair and added that she was always made to wear a white starched apron over her dress despite the fact that on the dray behind her were stacked innumerable bags of coal and slack. School-days were never the happiest days of her life she said, for class distinction was exercised in the classroom to some noticeable degree. It was felt that the children of the village notables were taken aside and encouraged while those whose father happened to be a ploughman or coal deliveryman were not given quite the same attention.

Nevertheless, before they left school all the children had been taught how to read, write and tackle a mathematical problem and this was considered to have been a satisfactory achievement both from the parents and school teacher's point of view.

When they left their new home at Skinner's Lock each morning, Wilfred cycled along the canal towpath to wherever he was working or reported to the maintenance gang's cabin based in the canal-side outbuildings at Cropwell Bishop. Here all the materials were stored for repairing lock-gates and maintaining the bridges to a satisfactory standard. The company's horses were also stabled here for they were still needed to pull the maintenance barges along the canal to their destination.

In those days the canal workers were employed by the L.N.E.R. (London North Eastern Railway) the company which also owned the canal. Every Friday afternoon all the men cycled from Cropwell Bishop to the station at Radcliffe-on-Trent to collect their pay packets.

Dolly, meanwhile, had found employment with the Braid Company Ltd situated on Aberdeen Street, Nottingham. Five mornings a week she walked the canal towpath to Tollerton Lane bridge and caught the five minutes to seven bus into the city.

She made many friends during her fourteen years spent with this company and in her lunch hour frequently shopped along Arkwright Street which extended from the Nottingham Midland Station to Trent Bridge. Among the main shops on and around this street Dolly found Frank Farrands, a large grocery concern with outlets throughout the city. Each of these branches was known as 'The Stores' to its regular stream of customers.

Here Dolly wrote out her grocery order in a small book, handed it over the counter and the goods were delivered by van to Skinner's Lock every other week. To get to the house the deliveryman had to park his vehicle at Peashill Farm then walk across two or three fields carrying a large box of groceries and often with the curious cattle hurrying in his wake.

Some household items Dolly brought home with her on the bus, but if they ran out of such items of food or wash powder, both she and her husband cycled out on Saturday mornings to a shop near the Cotgrave-Tollerton crossroads. They would set off with bags dangling from the handlebars of their 'boneshaker bicycles' and ride very carefully along the canal towpath which was then only a handlebar's width between the water's edge and the hedgerow. On reaching Tollerton Lane bridge they dismounted, wheeled the bicycles up the steep slope onto the road, turned right and rode again down to the crossroads. Here stood three farmworkers' cottages and the traditional corner shop. Dolly recalls this shop being so small that only one person could enter and be served at a time. So if you arrived on a morning of grey teeming rain you took shelter under the nearby elms if it was summer and got soaked in the autumn and winter when the trees were bereft of their foliage.

Wilfred and Dolly began to grow their own vegetables or bought them from the surrounding farms. The Bramley apple was a good source of fruit supply. Pears, plums, redcurrants and gooseberries could be bought at the one-person shop or from one of the larger corner shops in Cotgrave or Radcliffe-on-Trent.

Eggs were plentiful and almost every holding maintained a number of free range hens. In the season the eggs of moorhen and mallard were taken from the willow breaks in the Polser Brook and one egg removed from the nest of a green plover or lapwing when it was found.

Wilfred also walked over the fields to Peashill Farm to collect two or three pints of milk each week. These he carried in the rucksack slung over his shoulder and occasionally he would buy a few grocery items from a shop when he cycled home from the lengthmen's headquarters at Cropwell Bishop.

While he was hedging and ditching Wilfred also studied the rabbit runs and set his home-made snares accordingly. The surrounding countryside abounded in rabbits and at the weekends Dolly made pies and stews from the several rabbits her husband managed to snare each week. The skins would probably be sold to a local furrier. When he wasn't gardening, skinning rabbits or making snares Wilfred fished the stretch of canal close to the house. He caught perch, tench, bream and eels which, like most countrymen, he regarded as a rich delicacy although Dolly did not share his taste for these denizens of the canal bed and usually cooked something different for herself whenever her husband decided to have fried eel for his dinner or tea.

Summer evenings at the lock house were busy but seldom lonely; particularly at the weekends for on Friday evenings the local anglers would come up the towpath to fish overnight.

"Anglers would clamour around our back door on Friday and Saturday nights and I was kept busy filling their flasks with tea; at least until they settled down along the bank after dark." Dolly said when I was sitting on a bench outside the house wish her during a recent visit. After a few seconds' pause she continued: "In the morning they were there again, queueing up for breakfast. I used to cook them bacon, eggs and fried bread, give them a good strong mug of tea to go with it and charge them two or three pence each. Oh, aye. I had a nice little business going in those days.''

Because road and rail were becoming more popular modes of transport, the canal routes began to attract fewer barges and the Grantham Canal hosted its last barge in 1937. The L.N.E.R. then withdrew from managing the waterways and the Trent River. Board took over the repair, maintenance and conservation contracts. Fortunately the lengthmen were still employed in the same capacity and anglers continued to flank the towpath on warm summer evenings.

Then nature began to take over. The weed carpets thickened beneath the surface and fringes of reed, sedge and osier expanded into quite sizeable beds that attracted moorhens, coot and mallard in to feed, roost and breed. Smaller birds such as reed warblers and reed buntings were to be seen and much to Dolly's delight the kingfisher and heron. Occasionally a pair of mute swans would settle on the long pounds of water each side of Lock 4, so there was always something of interest to be seen or expected within a short walk of the lockhouse.

Asked if she could recall her experiences during the last war Dolly spoke of the horrors, bereavements and sadness caused by the bombings.

''We seemed to have had food rationing books and blackout curtains for years. Nor were we forgotten when it came to air raid shelters because all the lengthmen's houses along the thirty-three mile route were installed with these and although we didn't go running into them every night it was still comforting to know they were there.'' said Dolly.

She then mentioned one evening in particular. She was alone at the house and enjoying the peace and solitude of the surrounding countryside when suddenly an enemy aircraft appeared and began circling above the nearby Tollerton airfield which was an operational station during the war.

Dolly moving from room to room looked from the windows as the aircraft continued circling. Suddenly the pilot released a bomb which exploded across a tract of scrubland known as Thorntons Gorse. A second bomb was released over Cotgrave village before the pilot steered his machine onto a higher course and rejoined his squadron which was releasing bombs over Nottingham.

''It was terrifying. And very, very saddening. Because sixty-three souls lost their lives that evening,'' Dolly murmured sadly.

After the war, Wilfred continued his full-time task of canal lengthman while Dolly gave up working when she became pregnant. Just after the first baby was born, the water supply to the cottage was improved from the outlet that is piped beneath the lock house garden and empties into the Thurlbeck Dyke.

If one looks over the white picket fence as the dyke passes through the garden today he or she will see a flight of steps leading down to the water level. In years gone by a gate was affixed to the top of these steps to enable the lengthmen to go down to the water and clear any floating debris from its surface. He could also walk up to the sluice gates which he operated according to the water levels and amount of rainfall. The water surging down the Thurlbeck Dyke is that which is drained off from the surrounding farmland. To the right of the open channel water still pours from the pipe, and this Wilfred and Dolly were told, was pure drinking water.

The Skinners and the Waltons had always used this source for drinking but when Dolly gave birth to their son, Ernest, the Cotgrave lady who worked both as a nurse and voluntary midwife was doubtful as to its purity and also concerned because each time a jug or saucepan of water was needed either Wilfred or Dolly had to go out into rain, hail and snow and fill the vessel from the outlet opposite the steps.

When she was certain that mother and baby were otherwise comfortable in their waterside home the midwife approached a member of the Bingham Parish Council who had samples of this 'drinking water' sent to Boots' laboratories for analysis.

Within a matter of days, the Council received a report stating emphatically that the water was totally unfit for drinking. The appropriate section of the Trent River Board was approached and there followed several visits by both River Board and Council officials until eventually the house was connected to a full supply of usable water and the plumbings and fittings installed under the heading of 'modernisation'. No one is certain when the electricity mains were laid on at Skinner's Lock but for quite some years, and particularly during the Skinners and Waltons residency the rooms were lit by paraffin lamps.

In the summers to follow the lockhouse again resounded to the voices of two young children. The family also had a dog, cat and outdoor aviaries in which budgerigars and canaries were kept.

Being a more-or-less self-sufficient countryman, Wilfred's gift for making use of everything around him extended to collecting pieces of wood in all shapes and sizes and he became adept in the art of woodcarving. With his young family in mind he made little tables, chairs and toys. But, Dolly added, the family seemed to derive their greatest enjoyment from the set of skittles he carved and the perfectly rounded ball that was of course an essential part of the same unit.

Meanwhile, times were changing in the fields. The plough horse was facing redundancy as more and more farmers were investing in the new grey Fordson tractors. Cattle breeds were also losing favour and the traditional Shorthorns, Ayrshires and Lincolnshire Red Polls were being replaced by large herds of dual purpose Friesians.

The disused canal however continued to attract more waterfowl and both Wilfred and Dolly welcomed in their new neighbours; a fine pair of mute swans. Fifty or sixty years ago there was only a single breeding pair holding a territory between Lady Bay Bridge and Gamston. But the newcomers to the stretch of canal between Bassingfield and Skinner's Lock were encouraged to stay by all four members of the Bemrose family who fed bread and grain to the swans whenever they appeared within sight of the house.

Early one April morning the male or 'cob' began to build a nest at the foot of a sturdy elm rising from the bank opposite the lock house. The female or 'pen' eventually accepted this site and during the next fourteen days laid a clutch of seven eggs. This became an annual event and, after incubating the eggs for a further thirty five days, the swans usually hatched off five or six cygnets.

One season, Wilfred took a newly-laid egg from the nest and decided to have it for his tea. The contents apparently filled the bottom of a large frying pan. A ploughman also had the same idea but instead of taking a single egg he made off with the entire clutch.

When Wilfred came home at lunchtime he noticed that the pen was off the nest and went over the lock gate to find that the down lined hollow in which the eggs had been laid was empty. He then caught sight of a man ploughing the fields between the canal and Cotgrave Place and apprehended him.

The ploughman admitted to having stowed the eggs carefully into his rucksack but at Wilfred's request he returned all six to the nest. To the Bemrose family's delight the swans took to the water one morning with a brood of six fawnish grey cygnets bobbing buoyantly between them and Wilfred conceded that it was better to have six cygnets on a canal that six swan eggs resting on the cold slab of a ploughman's larder.

The swans became so tame that the cob frequently led his mate and cygnets into the lock house garden where they were continually fed on bread and grain. The cob also got the habit of tapping at the back door with the tip of his bill if none of his human benefactors were to be found in the garden. When the swan pair was beginning to nest for the ninth successive season the pen was shot by a lout. The cob eventually flew towards the Trent but did not return until the autumn. With him was a young pen. However, she did not take to the site as readily as his first mate and preferred the Bassingfield stretch of the canal although the pair failed to breed there.

Wilfred by this time had carved a life-sized mute swan out of wood. He painted it white, daubed its bill with dark red and the knob or berry at the base of the bill with black.

One morning he set his model beside the lock house and the resident cob came surging down with his wings fully arched over his back in readiness for battle. Even though the 'interloper' failed to move the cob regarded its shape and colourations as a threat and after splashing up over the bank proceeded to thrash it with his wings until Wilfred gently urged him aside and carried the model into the garden.

When I was a teenager in the 'fifties' I photographed a large cob swan with a young pen in tow at Bassingfield. As this cob was exceptionally tame I would say that, in all probability, he had been Wilfred and Dolly's immediate neighbour. Both swans left during that summer but since then various pairs have settled on the canal and attempted to breed. Some pairs have been very successful while others have suffered the cruelties administered by certain unbalanced members of the human race.

When the weather turned exceptionally cold and the canal surface was frozen from bank to bank, the swans flew toward the open waters of the Trent and most probably found a ready supply of food along its course.

The canal however was never totally deserted for the lengthmen still tramped through the snow checking for leaks and weak links in the lock-gates and at the weekends people came from Cotgrave and Radcliffe carrying their ice skates. Sunday afternoon was the most favoured time and I believe both Wilfred and Dolly skated alongside their children quite some distance along the waterway.

During such memorable snowfalls as those in 1947 and 1962/63 it was difficult for Wilfred and Dolly to trudge along the towpath or across the fields to the shops. But together they managed once or twice to walk to the small corner shop and struggle forcefully through the snow drifts carrying enough shopping to last them for a week or more. Later, friends ice skated up to the house where they received a warm welcome and in the summer a few families walked down the towpath from Cotgrave for the garden with its ornaments, flowing water, small bridges, apple trees and aviaries served as an attraction to young children whose visits were further highlighted when they discovered the cockatiels, romped around the garden or along the towpath with the dog or cat and fed the swans and cygnets that came up to the lock-gate for that precise purpose.

When Wilfred eventually retired, the British Waterways allowed the couple to remain at the house where they continued their rustic pursuits. By this time their children were married and bringing their own children to the house. Both

Wilfred and Dolly found themselves with a little more free time on their hands. But the sights and sounds of the surrounding countryside still pleasantly dominated their lives. If Dolly happened to see a kingfisher flashing swiftly and colourful as a thrown sapphire, she mentioned it to Wilfred.

If Wilfred heard the tawny owls hooting through the frost darkened stillness of a winter night he mentioned it to Dolly. Wishing to record something of the scene around his home Wilfred bought a single lens reflex camera and among the photographs he took were two really splendid shots of a mute swan pen standing over her eggs and turning them with the tip of her bill.

When he reached seventy-five however Wilfred's health began to deteriorate and there were days, Dolly told me, when he wanted to do little else but stay in bed. He began eating less and eventually accepted the advice of a lady doctor who suggested that he spend some time in hospital.

Sadly, it was here that he died quietly in his sleep and although Dolly lives at the cottage today it is still very much the way it was when her husband was alive, although the Thurlbeck Brook is now cut off from the natural bankings of the garden by a deep wall and a hard-core surface has been laid over the towpath so that Dolly's son and daughter can drive carefully beside the waterway when they take their children to visit their grandmother. There are still canaries and cockatiels in the garden aviaries and Ben, the friendly dog and Fluff the reclusive cat.

Wrens sing from the briars. Robins and blackbirds visit the garden and summer migrants like whinchats and yellow wagtails frequent the towpath and bordering hedgerows.

Tawny owls can still be heard calling in the darkness and most years a pair of mute swans tenant the waterway and rear a brood of cygnets. Mallard also rear their ducklings in the reedbeds.

Dolly has a word for everyone who walks the towpath and enjoyable have been the times when Tony Stevenson and I have joined her on the bench beside the white picket fence where she has usually enthused about a heron, kestrel or kingfisher that came within sight of the house a few days before our visit or chosen to quietly reminisce about her life spent with Wilfred at their home by Skinner's Lock.

TWO BROTHERS FROM CROMWELL BISHOP

George and Harold Smith were born in a slate-roofed cottage situated close to the church in Gropwell Bishop. The cottage was built in 1906 and when the family moved in their father lost no time in planting the adjacent plot with fruit trees and installing coops to which his free range hens returned each night.

Filled with the natural curiosity of all country boys, the brothers were turning over stones and looking for insects on the undersides almost as soon as they could walk. Summer days were spent birdnesting and chasing butterflies but on dark winter evenings they were often content to sit around the fire listening to the stories told or read to them by their mother or father.

These stories each parent interspersed with their personal anecdote and recollection, the most vivid perhaps concerning the boys' father who, in his younger days, was apprenticed to the firm of Walkers Agricultural Drill Mace at Tythby, a village which lies two miles south of Bingham.

One dusk, apprentice Smith was returning with a team engaged in the carting of timber from Belvoir Woods to the sawmills at Holme Pierrepon on the Earl Manvers estate, when it was realised that a crosscut saw had been left in the woods.

Fortunately the carters discovered this when they reached Langar and 'young Smith' was sent back to retrieve it, while the carters continued along the road with their haul of timber.

Having located the saw the boy had to return across the darkened fieldpaths to Tythby, install the saw into its rightful place, then take the diagonal path over the fields to the family home in Cropwell Bishop.

The fact that the saw had been left entailed him in a walk of about eight miles, yet the following morning he reported for work at first light, but with the intention of counting the tools when they were laid out in a woodland glade, so that he could ensure the same number was collected before the carters began the homeward journey about an hour before each dusk.

Another fireside anecdote concerned the boys' grandparents, their grandfather being employed as farm bailiff at Stragglethorpe, which was owned by the James family who were also the owners of nearby Cotgrave Place.

Situated within the farm outbuildings were a blacksmith's shop and forge and this is possibly the place where the boy's father mastered the craft involved in hammering out and shaping lengths of molten hot iron.

Grandfather Smith used regularly to drive a pony and gig to Nottingham market where his wife sold pounds and half pounds of oblong-shaped, hommade butter and new-laid eggs from a stall, in what was once the market place but which is now Slab Square.

The couple used to stable the pony and park the gig in a yard adjacent to the Black Boy Hotel. Harold remembers his mother telling him of an incident which occurred on a dark winter's evening when the couple were driving the pony and gig along what is now the A6011 road, between Gamston Bridge and Stragglethorpe. Suddenly a man leapt out from the ditchside shadows and hoisted himself over the back of the gig in an attempt to grab the day's takings which were secured in a cash box.

Startled, the farm bailiff pushed the pony into a trot, while his wife grabbed a meat cleaver, which they kept hidden in the front of the gig and reaching back she struck hastily at the man's hands. Obviously, the lady's only purpose was to frighten the thief, but the next day when they were sweeping out the gig, they discovered the flesh and blood stubs of his finger ends which they quickly swept aside.

Eventually, Grandfather Smith resigned from his position of farm bailiff and decided to embark upon his own cart carrier business, while still retaining the stall holder permit for Nottingham market. Grandmother Smith began to bake loaves of bread which she sold to the villages of Gropwell Bishop along with the new laid eggs. She was also tested for and acquired a midwife's certificate and duly delivered a number of healthy babies into the village community.

Her husband, in the meantime, conveyed people from one village to another in his carrier cart, collecting shopping for the sick and housebound and transporting furniture, carpets and various domestic items when a village family happened to be moving house.

Standing market in Nottingham also helped Grandfather Smith to make many friends and acquaintances, some of whom were eminent businessmen. One such a gentleman was a proprietor of a dressmaker's business based in Nottingham's Lace Market and Grandfather Smith was soon collecting and delivering 'out work' to the village folk.

Harold remembers the 'out work' comprising of boxes of beads. Both the adults and the children fitted these beads to the dresses that Grandfather Smith also brought home on the carriers cart and families spent many a winter evening engaged in 'bead sessions'.

The many dresses were probably hung on rails that were installed within the cottage, but the boxes of beads were kept in a padlocked shed, known simply as the 'bead shed', which had been erected close to the hen runs on a small section of the Smith's rear garden. Most families were engaged in this 'out work' at one time, but although it never produced a mint of wealth, it did of course provide them with a steady and alternative income.

When, in their formative years, George and Harold discovered the nooks and crannies of their village, they spent some hours playing boyhood games around the pinfold. This enclosure was believed to have been built in the seventeenth century and its purpose was that of all pinfolds namely, to house straying animals such as cows, sheep, pigs and horses, but even in the early part of this century people dumped litter around places that had been derelict and the Cropwell Bishop pinfold was no exception. Harold remembered it as being 'A place filled with nettles, sodden cardboard boxes, empty tins and bottles'.

Situated in the brickyard alongside the Grantham canal Cotton's chimney soared skyward and guided the boys about two hundred yards along the road from Cropwell Bishop to the A46 Fosse Way near their grandparent's original home in the village.

From Cotton's brickyard, each consignment of bricks was loaded onto a horse-drawn barge and conveyed to the canal's termination point near Lady Bay. Here the horses were unharnessed and led along the riverside, across Trent Bridge to the lock-gated entrance of the Nottingham Canal at London Road. Meanwhile, the barges were each attached to a strong length of cable spanning the width of the River Trent. Such an attachment ensured that the barges stayed in line and prevented them from drifting off-course during a particularly strong current. The bricks were finally off-loaded at one of the main wharves in the centre of Nottingham and loaded onto dreys hired by the builders merchants, whose next task was to ensure that each consignment was delivered on time to the increasing number of building sites.

While recalling their school-days, Harold remembers all the village school-masters. The village school was first opened in 1878 and the master elected in pioneering the way for his successors was William Parkin, who came from Sheffield. He retired in 1921 and was always keen to point out that he still had his own teeth. He died in December 1944 aged 89 and is buried in the village churchyard.

His successor, Mr Grainger, was a genial man who in his spare time worked as a volunteer for the British Legion. He also ran a magazine club in which each edition of 'Wide World' was eagerly awaited by almost every member.

The third in the line of schoolmasters was undoubtedly the most formidable so far as the boys were concerned. An ex-sergeant major who had seen action in the First World War, he was strict to the last letter and frequently caned boys who misbehaved or were careless.

Harold remembers one schoolmate being quite brilliant at mathematics but who, one afternoon, allowed ink to drop from his pen nib onto the page of his exercise book. This the schoolmaster regarded as a misdemeanour and in seemingly no time he had the boy out in front of the class and was thrashing his bare buttocks with a cane.

As the brothers grew older, their wanderings extended beyond the village to the surrounding countryside where George, in particular, set snares to catch rabbits and became the friend of several gamekeepers, due to his willingness to help them rid the estates and coverts of the many rabbits thriving there.

Carrying purse nets and a couple of ferrets, young George studied the runs and ground contours on each estate and also won the respect of the woodsmen and estate stewards, who encouraged him to work towards the tasks he would one day be undertaking on a full-time basis.

Harold, meanwhile, explored the coverts with another purpose in mind for he was greatly interested in local history. At a relatively early age, he had learned how the 'Enclosure Act' had originated and how the fox-hunting vogue, which gained tremendous popularity among the titled folk in the eighteenth century, had changed the landscape to some noticeable degree.

Close to Cropwell Bishop stands Hoe Hill which was bare hillside until around 1831. It was then that the famous squire, Jack Chaworth Musters, decided to plant the topmost knoll of Hoe Hill with trees and hawthorns purposely to serve as coverts for the foxes.

Several artificial earths were dug and lined with brick and this small monument to times gone by provides habitat for foxes and a variety of small wild birds to this day.

Harold also discovered that three woods at nearby Colston Bassett, were owned by Sir Edward Le Marchant who had named them after each of his daughters: Winifred, Blanche and Kaye. These woods were also planted for use as coverts and artificial earths were established accordingly.

On leaving school, George acquired employment at the British Gypsum Works, but never lost his prowess for working with the purse nets, ferrets and terriers. He yearned for a gamekeeper's position which then appeared to be far and few between. Then on the countryman's grapevine came news of a vacancy on Lord Belper's estate close to the Nottinghamshire-Derbyshire border. Along with seventy-one other applicants, George duly wrote a letter stating his interest in the vacancy and enclosed within the envelope a reference given by local gamekeeper Mr Ward. To George's obvious delight, he was invited to attend an interview held in the office of a building attached to Lord Belper's residence at Kingston Hall.

Fox cubs were occasionally reared by the gamekeepers and staff of a country estate.

Nor were many days to pass before he received a letter formally offering him the position of underkeeper which he gratefully accepted. Harold, on consulting his diary for the year 1935, noted that the cost of transporting his brother's furniture and belongings the sixteen miles from Cropwell Bishop to Kingston upon Soar was one pound and ten shillings. What, we have wondered, would it cost today?

With Harold working at British Gypsum, then changing his occupation to that of Lorry driver for Blue Circle Cement, George merged gratefully into a countryside occupation and, in seemingly no time, was enjoying life as an underkeeper.

Excluding George, the keeper's staff numbered five. Serving under a head-keeper, their daily schedule began with a check of all the traps that had been set throughout the estate. Each keeper was allocated a particular beat and the trap inspections had to be carried out before nine.

Quite a variety of birds and animals were regarded as vermin in George's day and the variously shaped and designed traps accounted for a number of foxes, stoats, weasels and the occasional hedgehog or red squirrel.

All birds regarded as a threat to the broods of pheasant chicks were shot and such a list of feathered vermin included jay, magpie, carrion crow, sparrow-hawk, kestrel, little owl, tawny and barn owl. Barn owls were quite prolific throughout the Trent and Soar valleys when George was a lad and quite a number were caught on the pole traps that were staked out with the hope that a bird of prey would settle to perch there, thus setting off the spring which clamped its taloned feet to the trap and often left the bird fluttering upside down to await its inevitable end. This, of course, was a cruel form of regulating the number of predators in one area, but George had to undertake the task in the same way as anyone similarly employed.

Some days he worked the rabbit warrens with his ferrets and beloved terriers, but the main task revolved around the rearing of pheasants to provide game for the gentry throughout the autumn and winter shooting seasons.

Every three or four days, therefore, the keeper patrolled the woods on his beat, watched the hen pheasants and discovered where they were nesting. He then notched the trees or bushes beside each nest and when the pheasant left to feed, he would go round the nests, remove the eggs and gently put each in the bag which was strapped around his shoulders. The eggs he would then take back to the rearing field and two or three at one time would be placed under each of the brooding hens restrained within a rearing coop. When the pheasants returned to their empty nests, they simply settled in to lay more eggs and two or three days later, the keeper would return and collect them up.

The shooting parties first assembled in September when the grey or common partridges were the main quarry. Glossy field sports magazines were describing the Nottinghamshire fields and coverts as 'partridge rich', therefore the keepers of the estates were duty bound to rear as many chicks as possible and have them on the wing long before the first chills of autumn settled across the coverts.

Pheasant shooting lasted from October to January, and on the Kingston estate two day shoots were held every two weeks. Kingston was regarded in fact as one of the best pheasant shoots in England during the 1930s and many distinguished guests visited Lord Belper's estate. The traditional "stewards' day" or "family day" was also included in the sporting itinerary; the latter taking place on Boxing Day 'to blow away the cobwebs, whisky, gin and cigar smoke'

On recalling one or two colourful incidents, George mentions the end of a particularly hard winter in which the ice layering the park lake was just beginning to thaw.

Lord and Lady Belper were standing on the snow frozen banks watching their small flock of pinioned Canada geese cross the ice when her Ladyship's two cairn terriers bounded onto the surface. One returned to the Belper's the moment its name was called, but the second disappeared suddenly, much to the couple's distress. Turning in sudden desperation, Lord Belper saw the man who was in charge of his game carts walking up the drive and duly shouted him over and then asked him to go in and get the dog. But the 'gamecart man' as he was known, could not swim and so Lord Belper quickly discarded his own heavy overcoat, handed it to the gamecart man and dived into the lake.

The cairn he rescued just in time and as a soaking wet, but jubilant figure, he returned to his distraught wife clutching the dog. Flinging the overcoat around his shoulders, Lady Belper helped her husband across the snow to the Hall where a hot bath and a bottle of whisky became the next items on his Lordship's agenda.

George, incidentally, had already married his Cropwell Bishop girlfriend when he moved to Kingston. The couple also had one son and two more sons were born during his stay there. Occasionally George was asked by his employer to join the keepers on the nearby Whatton House estate which was owned by Lord Crawshaw. Here, his task was to help round up the herd of fallow deer by using grey hounds to bring in the outliers.

One or two of the finer bucks and does were driven into pens and from there transported to other country estate owners, who intended to maintain a herd of deer within their grounds. The deer were, of course, sold in the same manner as other forms of livestock.

While out in the villages, George would sometimes hear about the sizeable badger sett which was established at nearby Thrumpton although the Kingston pheasants' coverts were seldom ravaged by badgers and even fewer foxes, for these animals were kept in check due to a continual process of trapping.

In common with most large country estates, Kingston had its problems with the local poaching fraternity, most of whom journeyed from Nottingham to the estate in a convoy of small vans, but usually entered the private grounds by the tunnel close to Radcliffe Lock.

When poachers were caught, as they occasionally were, there was no violence, even though they faced a three-month prison sentence. One or two even cycled back to the estate after a spell of imprisonment and talked to the gamekeeper about game, wildlife and country lore in general.

George remembers the night they pursued a really well-built man, who in the darkness stumbled and fell into a ditch. Ready to meet the onslaught of his fists when he rose from the mud and slurry, George and his workmates surrounded the ditch, but were amazed when the man turned over onto his back and burst out laughing, while indicating at the same time that he would come quietly.

Ever vigilant, the local gamekeepers passed word among themselves that a man had begun cycling daily from Long Eaton to West Leake with a twenty bore gun strapped to the crossbar of his bicycle. Although a slender gun, George was quick to point out that one could shoot anything with it and so it became obvious that the man intended taking home the occasional brace of pheasant or partridge, which might have strayed from the hedgerow to take grit from the side of the road.

The keeper, on the neighbouring estate at West Leake, learned somehow that when the cyclist reached his place of work, the gun was not to be seen and so the keeper rightly concluded that he hid it in a covert or wood. After diligently combing their beats, one of the keepers found the twenty bore hidden in the undergrowth of a wood at Thrumpton, but the man never was apprehended. Instead the keeper removed the gun and nothing was heard of the matter.

George was employed on the Kingston estate for four years before he moved to Appleby in, what was then known as, Westmorland. Here his life became equally as interesting but does not relate to the country as this book does. However, I will mention the fact that George was at Appleby when war broke out and he enlisted for Army service, but after a year was found to be suffering from a duodenal ulcer and ultimately discharged. He returned to the Appleby estate until 1949, then learned of another vacancy in his natal county.

His next employer was Colonel Foreman Hardy whose mother owned Widmerpool Hall deep in the hunting shires, and again, quite close to the Nottinghamshire/Leicestershire border.

George by this time was deeply involved with working terriers, spaniels and labradors while undertaking the annual routine expected of a competent game keeper. His routine at Widmerpool was basically the same as that undertaken on the previous estates, except that George was able to widen his experience by embarking on the occasional duck-shooting foray and in the season travelling up to the Derbyshire 'grouse moors fortnight' for a day's shooting from the butts.

When turning out for a Widmerpool pheasant shoot one bitterly cold January morning, Colonel Foreman Hardy took George aside and asked him to peruse his shooting attire. "Can you see any striped garments peeping out anywhere?", the Colonel asked.

"No Sir".

"Good. Because I am still wearing my pyjamas under this lot", the colonel replied before turning to welcome his guests.

George took particular interest in building up the number of common partridge in the area while still keeping the predators at bay. He kept a wary eye on the activities of the badgers which were well established in the banks of the stonepit quarry opposite the Hall and being on the edge of the countryside hunted over by the Quorn, he still had to conserve a fair sprinkling of foxes as well as provide good numbers of pheasants.

Careful management, however, resulted in both pheasants and foxes thriving admirably within the coverts of Widmerpool Hall and in 1954 George received a letter from the Quorn huntsman Dennis Aldridge, who as also an artist and friend of Lionel Edwards, the famed artist whose valued canvases are displayed in the lounges and halls of many fine country seats and farmhouses to this day. The letter, written when the hunting season had come to a close, read as follows:

The letter was written in appreciation of the help and cooperation extended whenever the Quorn hunted across the Windmerpool estate and emphasized the fact that careful management can result in pheasants and foxes living together. George kept this letter and was keen to show it to anyone wanting to talk with him about field sports and conservation. He received many such accolades throughout his career and I had heard about George from such friends as Jim, the warrener and Forestry Commission Ranger, long before I met him.

When the Colonel died, the management of the estate continued but with the Hall standing empty and awaiting a new occupant. Fortunately, the practice rearing pheasants and partridges continued and foxes were still being encouraged to breed within the coverts. On one occasion, George discovered a nursing vixen dead at the side of the road and spent that day searching for the earth into which he carefully dug and recovered the litter of four or five cubs. Those mites he reared on goats' milk, kitchen scraps and dog food. When they were four or five weeks old, he placed them in a disused pigsty and fed them from the trough. His brother Harold, who was visiting one afternoon, recalls the cubs lined up and gulping down small nodules of dog food laced with goats' milk, while each had its tiny tail uplifted and wagging in the manner of a puppy or piglet.

Once the cubs were old enough to fend for themselves, George released them into the surrounding coverts and none, so far as he was aware, returned to the pig yard attached to the Hall.

Experience and an easy-going disposition won George many friends, among whom were men interested in breeding terriers, spaniels and labradors. Thus his professional network widened and he was eventually invited to attend working terrier shows and gun dog trials. In fact, at the age of eighty-two, he was still attending them.

Before it was banned in Nottinghamshire, George also enjoyed otter hunting, but he explained, it was not being in at the kill that interested him, but exploring the tracts of countryside and river valleys that were new to him. He was met at Widmerpool by a policeman with a similar wanderlust and the two men drove out to meets at Thoresby, Welbeck, Clumber. Blythe and Serlby where the biggest dog otter to be taken by the local pack of otter hounds was found.

Since otter hunting was banned in Nottinghamshire during the mid-sixties, George has seen a quite sizeable dog otter on the small island close to the buttresses of the Classical Bridge in Clumber Park, where it remained searching for food until the voices of a family approaching the bridge were cause enough for it to enter the water and turn downstream towards the chapel.

When George left Widmerpool for his present position at Winkburn near Southwell, the Hall again changed hands and became the home of the Walker family who were agents for the Wolseley car. In later years however, Widmerpool Hall became the administrative centre for the Automobile Association and remains so to this day.

Although George was in his early eighties, he still worked as a part-time keeper and looked after terrier bitches in whelp, kept an eye on the partridge, pheasant and fox populations and was always keen to show photographs from his private collection that depict shooting parties and countryside events. When the Game Fair was held at Welbeck, George received a medal, awarded by the Country Landowners Association, for forty years spent employed as a game-keeper on two Nottinghamshire estates.

I was privileged to have met George about two years before he died. The interior of his lodge was hung with sporting prints, paintings and photographs of working terriers and trophies such as a fox mask and brush, and a pair of roebuck antlers. Items of memorabilia adorned every nook and cranny, and most items George rightly regarded as the harvest of his long career.

Harold still lives in the cottage in which he was born. With a lifelong interest in birdlife and the countryside, he still retains the orchard attached to the cottage and keeps poultry within its walled confines. "Mine is the only cottage in the village that has still an orchard attached to it. The other orchards and similar plots of ground have been sold off for building purposes,'' my friend explained sadly.

I was surprised to learn that Harold was also the local Methodist preacher. ''I had such a bad time in the last war that I said to myself that if I ever returned home unscathed it would be a miracle – and miracles you can only relate to God. I also made a pact that I would spread God's word as frequently as I could and when I saw the steeple of Cropwell Bishop church after many nightmare skirmishes in occupied France, I had visited the vicar within days of unpacking my suitcase'.

As you walk or drive slowly with him through the village, he points to the newly built houses and says; ''That's where the blacksmith and farriers used to be and on that site there was once a mill where my father worked for a short time before he too became a blacksmith''.

Every corner of the village is home to Harold and every covert, field path and woodland glade, the bygone workshop in which George has learned his trade and passed it on to others.

Both men held fast to the hard but unhurried theme of times gone by, and this fact became even more apparent on the afternoon I spent at Winkburn with these two brothers from Cropwell Bishop.

FOOTNOTE

In October 1991, George took his friend and daily helper aside and told her that he would be dead within the next three days. Nor was his personal prophecy without foundation for inside that span of time he died in his sleep at the age of eighty-three.

At the funeral service held in Winkburn church many country folk came from far and wide to pay their respects. There was not a single empty pew, in fact people were standing at the back of the church. The coffin bearers were four red-coated members of the local hunt, the Grove and Rufford and, when the service was over, a member of the South Notts hunt stood in the church porch, raised the hunting horn to his lips, and blew 'Gone Away' as the old gamekeeper's friends and mourners stood with heads bowed while they acknowledged the passing of a loyal companion and traditional countryman.

BY CHARABANC TO SHERWOOD

In the early 1920s, or perhaps some little time before, the landlords and stewards of both public houses and workers institutes began to organise charabanc outings into Derbyshire and the Robin Hood Country, or the Nottinghamshire 'Dukeries', as north Nottinghamshire was then known.

The first tour operators were also visualising weekend trips throughout the region and one brochure I was given begins thus: 'What imagery is conjured up in the mind by mention of a holiday ramble through the Dukeries. What recollections of a happy day crowd into the memory of those who have enjoyed the glories of the woodland scenery, and what pleasures, yet unrealized, are there in store for the weary sojourner in murky cities, anticipating a tour through the forest glades where nature invites the toil-worn traveller to breathe her freshest, purest zephyrs, wafting on the air the scents of a thousand perfumed flowers, gay with harmonious hues'. My goodness!

The murky cities mentioned were obviously Nottingham, Derby, Sheffield and Manchester. But tours were also being operated from the smaller towns as can be gleaned from the following advertisement:

Retford Motor Services Ltd
27 Grove Street
Retford.
Tel 220
Tour the glorious country of England's Dukeries. Parties may book special saloons for any outing. Travel from Doncaster, Worksop, Nottingham and Retford to Edwinstowe by Direct Service.

From Worksop, we read of:

W Rains
Job Master and Hiring Contractor

Operating from Watson Road and Victoria Mews, this gentleman offered 'First class carriages of every kind for large or small parties. Good careful and competent drivers. By kind permission of various noblemen, W Rains has the privilege of holding keys and passes, thus enabling his patrons to visit all the Private Drives etc.'

The Portland Garage Worksop advertised as 'Charabanc and Taxi Hire Specialists' and offered their potential customers to: 'Let us quote for your trips around the Dukeries – Luxurious Chara's and Competent Drivers. Trains met at Worksop by appointment. Taxis for Hire'.

The Normanton Inn, c. 1910. (Photography: C. Shaw)

Meanwhile, the hoteliers were not slow in offering accommodation for motorists and charabanc weekenders. The White House Ollerton and the Clarence Temperance Worksop were soon advertising their facilities, the latter also offering the additional use of Bartnops Comfortable Taxis which met the trains at Worksop. The Normanton Inn, Clumber Park, was recorded as 'A Hotel recommended by the Automobile and Motor Union Association', with Mrs Mary J Sadler, the Proprietress, 'welcoming all visitors'. This hostelry was advertised as 'situated amidst the most beautiful Peak and Forest Scenery in the Kingdom. A few minutes walk from the celebrated Beech and Lime Tree Avenues and a short and pleasant walk from Clumber House and Church! It catered for families each requiring a private sitting room, or parties needing large rooms in which to hold meetings or have dinner. Among the outbuildings was good stabling with loose boxes and a motor garage with the added luxury of an inspection pit.

All around the Dukeries, hotel menus began to feature such gastronomical delights as jugged hare, roast pheasant, haunch of venison roasted on a spit, beef, lamb, pork, and from Budby roast swan, 'delicious and well browned'.

George Morrison Pearce, who was proprietor of the Black Swan Hotel Edwinstowe, offered large rooms well able to accommodate parties of two hundred people. Everything would be provided at short notice and attached to the site was a grass field where small fetes and galas could be held as well as games of cricket, tug of war and pitching the horse shoe.

Some fine cars were soon to be seen travelling the forest roads among them being the Rover, Daimler, Standard, Armstrong-Siddeley, Talbot and Chevrolet.

Fancy goods dealers such as Sisson and Son of Bridge Street Worksop, advertised their leather goods and perfumes. Freestone and Sons of Victoria Square, Worksop advertised their special brand of malt bread, and decorated cakes for 'weddings, Birthdays and all occasions'.

An Edwardian ice-cream seller. (Photograph: C. Shaw)

B. Shipside 'The largest and most up to date garage in the district' then situated in Newcastle Avenue, stated that urgent repairs were a speciality and additionally that they were agents for Morris, Singer, Jowett and Chrysler cars.

Also capitalising in the Dukeries first tourist boom were the ice cream sellers, particularly Higgins of Worksop, whose salesmen drove cars that looked something like mobile roundabouts, wore peaked caps and white smocks and offered their top quality Ice Cream Deluxe. The Sinclairs who ran the Post Office in Edwinstowe were equally keen to advertise the fact that they were also tobacconists, stationers and the proprietors of a sizeable lending library. Postcard views of the Dukeries could be obtained from Sisson & Son, Bridge Street, Worksop, who also became the stockists for local ordnance maps, motorists' maps and guides.

Photographs of the Dukeries and portraits or studies of family and social groups were to be arranged by conferring with 'All Kodak Requisites'.

Thus, the scene was set. Everyone it seems could be catered for in the heart of greenest Sherwood.

Welbeck Abbey was situated three miles away from the main road, therefore the tourist saw avenues of trees, chains of lakes and all kinds of grazing cattle, sheep and deer long before they finally viewed the house. From Welbeck they took the highway that runs between the estates of the Duke of Newcastle on the left-hand and the Duke of Portland on the other. Their route then continued through Carburton flanked by the delightful roadside lakes and then wound uphill to Budby Common, from whence 'a fine panoramic view of woods and moorland presents itself.' From there, the cavalcades travelled the short distance to Budby, a small but beautiful village connected to the Thoresby Estate. Then along the undulating road to Ollerton Corner, where 'one of the most delightful prospects in Merrie Sherwood may be seen. There the motorist would do well to leave his car and saunter through the glorious Beech Avenues, the long dark aisles of which resemble those of an ancient cathedral. From Ollerton the journey may be continued via the by-pass road to Edwinstowe near to which historic village, the Major Oak, one of the largest trees in England, reigns in sylvan state. The car may be parked in the forest whilst the occupants wander along the shady walks, take in the beauties of the Birklands and if time permits obtain a glimpse of the curious Archway Lodge near Clipstone where King John had a hunting palace.'

On leaving Edwinstowe the tourists were obliged to take one of two routes. They could either return to Ollerton and by-pass the new Thoresby Colliery or go directly through Edwinstowe village to the cross roads near Rufford Abbey. Turning left they would then travel the winding route to Ollerton or take the road to Perlethorpe close to the boundaries of Thoresby Park. This road was often favoured because it terminated close to the Normanton Inn. Although the leaflets distributed by the guides suggested that they continue along to 'Apley Head, a favourite rendezvous for motorists from the big towns'.

Apley Head Lodge was the formal entrance into Clumber Park and is still regarded as such for that matter. There are several intersecting routes leading to and from the lake and woods but the main lime avenue-is about four miles long and terminated at Carburton. Clumber had much to offer for its house was still standing, the River Poulter, by then referred to as 'a great lake', attracted many species of waterfowl and in May the flowering thickets of rhododendrons were 'pure delight to the eye'.

From Carburton, the charabancs or taxis crossed the main Ollerton-Worksop road and proceeded for a short way along the Cuckney road until they found a parking spot from there they could again view the Carburton Lakes. The road borders Welbeck Park where 'glorious views of woods and water are unfolded'. Having arrived at the tiny village of Cuckney the tourists turned alongside the church and took the route sign-posted for Budby. The leaflet informed them that 'This is a remarkably pretty road, the interlacing branches of the overhanging trees form a leafy tunnel'.

At Budby the journey continued across the main Ollerton-Worksop road and access was given to allow the vehicles along the road which cuts directly through Thoresby Park. This route eventually became a public road and can be regarded as such to this day.

The homeward trek took the sightseers by Apley Head and the woods and forest glades of Manton to Worksop. Or as the leaflet pointed out 'Another pleasant road is that from Budby to Edwinstowe. The distance in only short, but the way lies through the most ancient part of the forest'.

Once the trips were over, the hoteliers, kitchen staff, servants, valets and butlers were summoned to their duties which revolved around making their guests comfortable and exploring the prospects of returning to North Nottinghamshire.

The charabanc organisers drew up a list of rules and regulations relating to the houses and grounds which they were privileged to visit. Quite a number of these regulations were continuously being received from the estate stewards who acted on behalf of the estate owners, and eventually the organisers collated these and produced a leaflet entitled:

SHERWOOD FOREST AND THE DUKERIES ESTATES, HINTS TO VISITORS

WELBECK ABBEY – *Regulations in force in pre-war years have been cancelled and Welbeck Abbey Pleasure Grounds, Gardens and Riding School are closed to the public.*
The drives through the Birklands are likewise closed to the public. Motor vehicles of any description are strictly prohibited on the private roads.

CLUMBER PARK – *Clumber House is not shown to visitors.*
The interior of the church can be viewed on Monday and Thursday from 10 am to 4 pm on presentation of ticket obtainable from the Estate Office, Worksop. Tickets for Sunday Services (10 am to 6 pm) are also issued. Clumber Park is open to the public on Monday, Thursday and Saturday by permit to be obtained from the Agent at Newcastle Estate Office, Worksop. It should also be noted that all rules and regulations apply equally to cyclists and passengers as well as to horse-drawn vehicles.

THORESBY PARK – *Thoresby Park is open to the public on Monday, Thursday and Saturday only. The private road which may be used is the one leading from Edwinstowe to the Buck Gates, past Thoresby House to Clumber South Lodge and vice versa.*
On all other private roads are notice-boards 'No Motor Cars or Motor Cycles allowed' and this regulation is strictly enforced.
Thoresby House is not shown to visitors.
All rules and regulations apply equally to cyclists and foot passengers as well as to horse-drawn vehicles – that is, they must not traverse the private roads other than indicated. Visitors to the Major Oak must walk from the hard roads as vehicles are not allowed to be driven to the tree.

NOTE
The privilege of driving visitors on certain private roads (by horse drawn vehicles only) is confined to members of the Dukeries Posting Proprietors Association, applications should be made to Mr W Rains, Watson Road, Worksop.
Though most private roads to the Dukeries are closed to motor vehicles there are numerous beauty spots accessible and visitors cannot do better than put themselves in the hands of the motor car and charabanc proprietors who operate tours throughout the region.

LIFE AROUND THE COUNTRY HOUSE

Nottinghamshire has for centuries nurtured a succession of titled families whose ancestors were granted, or acquired, sizeable tracts of land upon which they usually maintained a number of tenant farms. Their own house or country seat was often situated within the pole fenced or walled confines of a park with a formal or 'grand' avenue leading directly from an ornately designed gate-lodge to the main entrance of the house which, to the villagers, was always known as The Hall.

All the gateways leading in to a park were kept locked and if someone had to enter for business reasons they were required to ring a bell.

One of the gatekeeper's family would then appear and ask if the visitor had an appointment while enquiring at the same time as to the nature of their business.

If by some mischance the gatekeeper had not been told that the caller was expected, there was no way in which he or she could enter the park, for the gatekeeper's family were loyal and not likely to offend their landlord and employer by admitting a hawker or someone who might become a persistent nuisance.

Beyond the gate-lodge the trees planted either side of the formal avenue were usually lime. Imported from the Netherlands they were considered to be the best tree species suited to blend in with the parklands surrounding a country seat. Being members of the tea bush family they were also relatively fast growing trees, although the midsummer foliage becomes consistently sticky due to the intervention by aphids.

John Evelyn in his book 'Sylva', published in 1664, praised the lime tree to such an extent that the landowners acquired them specifically for the purpose of producing a leafy bower or 'arbour' aspect to those travelling the avenue, either as a layman tied by occupation to the estate or a visiting peer glimpsing green vistas through the windows of a horse drawn coach or chauffeur driven Rolls Royce.

A group of valets in traditional country-house dress. (Photograph: F.Parkes)

Nor was the word 'avenue' relating to the French verb 'avenir' used in an idle sense. Its English interpretation denotes arrival or approach and again, in his 'Sylva', John Evelyn gave an explanatory list of words which he considered unfamiliar to the average reader yet applicable to the text. An avenue he described as 'the principal walk to the front of the house or seat'.

By the time that the lime avenues on most estates were displaying full summer foliage, groves of horse chestnut trees had come into fashion, particularly around the 1750s and the vogue for different tree species seemed to change every fifty or seventy-five years. Consequently, the average country house could boast of having something like one hundred and thirty-five species planted across its parklands and by the early 1920s, the average formal garden usually contain ed stands of Maple, Acacia, Holme or evergreen Oak, Monkey Puzzle trees and Cedars of Lebanon, all of which competed with the water gardens and thickets of bamboo and rhododendron, at catching the visitor's eye.

Cedars were often planted around the edges of wide lawns. There is a sense of peace interpreted by the smoothness of grass and the shade of trees. In having said this, I am fairly well convinced that John Evelyn influenced many landowners in the belief that of all the trees planted throughout an estate, the cedars depicted both serenity and status. Evelyn wrote:

'But now after all the beautiful and stately trees clad in perpetual splendour shall I not forget the Cedar which grows in all extremes – for so it does on the mountains of Lebanon from whence I have received cones and seeds of those few remaining trees.'

Of Nottinghamshire's titled families, the Bentincks of Welbeck were best known to the villagers of the Sherwood Forest country in the same way that the Middletons of Wollaton were the family mentioned by almost everyone whose livelihood revolved around the centre of Nottingham and along to the Balloon Wood crossroads.

But there were many others – notably the Edges of Strelley, Coopers of Thurgaton, Chaworth-Musters of Annesley, Pierreponts of Holme Pierrepont and Thoresby, Sherbrookes of Oxton, Stanhopes of Rampton and Shelford and the Thoroton-Hildyards of Flintham, to name but a few. Most of these landowners had interesting pedigrees. Some were the descendants of families who had been granted sizeable tracts of land for their allegiance to King and Country during the eleventh and twelfth centuries. Others had married into the families of their descendants while a few such as the Bentincks could trace their thirteenth-century ancestors to Guelderland, Holland and it was not until 1688 that Hans-William Bentinck accompanied William III to England during the Revolution of that year and became the King's confidential adviser and diplomat before taking up the sword at the battle of Boyne; part of the Irish Campaign which was fought in 1690. Thus he was duly rewarded with a fine estate – but originally in Buckinghamshire.

His son, Henry, gained the title of Lordship of Titchfield in Hampshire after marrying Lady Elizabeth Noel, daughter of the Earl of Gainsborough. William, his son, then married Margaret Cavendish Harley who was the only daughter of the Earl of Oxford and he inherited the Welbeck House and estate in Nottinghamshire on the death of his mother-in-law, the Countess of Oxford, in 1755. This is but one example of how lands were acquired through marriage.

But the landowners were never idle. Quite a number became barristers, lawyers and diplomats as well as keen businessmen, each surrounded by a retinue of shrewd advisers. In many of these country houses portraits of the family's ancestors adorn the walls just as they did at the turn of the century when the less formal sections of each house provided employment for a varied and colourful staff, the majority of whom came from working-class backgrounds.

The occupants of a country house were divided into two social factions; family and servants. The servants, whatever their rank, were provided with accommodation, a uniform, food and of course, pay. Few were there among them who did not have the smooth running of the house and estate foremost in their minds for such was the nature of their duties.

The kitchens of the large country house were occupied longer and more consistently than other rooms within the building. Ovens built into wall units and stoves of black iron were in constant use. Copper pans seethed on the hobs. Steam rose to ceiling height and a newcomer would have no doubt enjoyed the aromas of herbs, fruit and boiled ham or bacon which the cooks themselves were seldom aware of because they were surrounded by such aromas throughout each working day.

The centre of the kitchen was occupied by two well-scrubbed tables placed together. At one end a maid could peel potatoes or slice swedes and carrots while at another, her workmate busied herself with the task of plucking pheasants, partridges and woodcock. The cook, who was always in charge, usually rolled out the pastry, organised the meals after having conferred each day with the lady of the house and instructed the maids in respect of filleting fish, mixing sauces and garnishing the variety of coldmeats or 'snacks'. Periodically, the cook would open the oven doors to check how the side of pork, crown of lamb or haunch of venison was progressing and if it appeared slow she would instruct the maids to stoke up the fire and keep an eye on it, while never once ignoring it herself.

Puddings were kept in the cold room and more often than not these had been baked or prepared and decorated a day or so beforehand except, of course, jellies and trifles.

After her morning coffee the housekeeper would go down to the kitchen and check with the cook in respect of everything being ready for the appointed hour. Any last minute changes were agreed upon by both senior women. But the cook usually had the last word for those kitchens were her occupational domain and few save the occasional butler or valet chose to loiter there for, in the words of one retired cook, "everybody was too blooming busy to spend time standing gossiping. So if anybody came who we thought would waste our time we saw 'em off and they soon got the hang of it".

His Lordship left all domestic matters to his wife who handed the responsibility to the housekeeper and she in effect was in charge of all the maids and supervised their duty roster accordingly.

I have interviewed several elderly ladies who were once employed as maids and they regarded the housekeeper as a 'kindly soul; almost a mother to you in a way. Yet she was never allowed to let things slide and was answerable to Her Ladyship's every request and whim throughout her term of employment'.

Most housekeepers stayed with a family for many years. Those who were seeking fresh positions were 'on the books' of several Domestic Agencies in Nottingham, Mansfield and Derby. I should add that a spinster seeking employment, perhaps after nursing an ailing parent, was preferred as opposed to a married woman who would normally, and quite naturally, put the needs of her own family before those of her employees. The housekeeper was expected to know everything about running the household. She was provided with an office – "the housekeeper's room" -and kept an accounts ledger as well as a shopping list pad and day-to-day diary. Everything from sacks of flour to packets of sultanas, gallons of paraffin for the lamps to barrels of treacle, were listed and checked.

Usually the cook made out the first list and had one of her girls deliver it to the housekeeper. But even then the housekeeper was never in. sole charge for the lists and accounts were inspected by Her Ladyship either weekly or monthly.

Most of the supplies were locked in a still room, the keys of which were usually hung from the clasp of the belt encircling the housekeeper's waist. When her accounts had been checked then she embarked upon a tour of inspection, checking that the windows were clean, the rooms tidy and the furniture and ornaments free from dust.

She would stop a maid and tell her to adjust her apron strap or straighten her cap. She would also advise as to where a certain needle and thread might be located.

After her tour, she usually retired to her room and rang the bell to indicate that she was waiting to be served with the morning cup of coffee. In many households the bell for each important member of staff was usually numbered and strung along one wall near the servants' room so that the summons would be answered immediately. The housekeeper conferred with the butler over morning coffee and further arrangements were made for that day and the week in hand.

The butler was head of the male indoor servants. His basic duties involved checking that his staff carried out their duties in an orderly manner and doubly ensuring that the guests were attended to according to the function taking place at a particular time. By the turn of the century, every middle class household employed servants but it was only in the houses of the more aristocratic families that men were employed in this capacity.

The cellars were the butler's domain. Here kegs of sherry and racks of wine were stored alongside bottles of port and claret. The port was poured into wide based decanters before being placed on the table. The claret he poured into crystal jugs which he tasted then set aside for a while until they had reached room temperature.

He was conscious of damask table-cloths, napkins, silver knives, forks, spoons, fruit bowls, condiment sets and candlesticks and throughout the day wore a smart morning suit. But, at six each evening, the butler changed into full evening dress with coat tails and black bow tie, his main task being to supervise the valets and footmen who served the family with dinner.

Usually he stood at the side of the table but, in winter, with his back to the roaring fire if he could, and by looking into a convex mirror, he would indicate to the footmen merely by discreetly nodding his head, which of the guests required a glass filling or a plate removed from the table.

His Lordship and Ladyship each employed a personal servant to help them dress and keep their rooms tidy.

The master's servant was known as a valet, while his wife was attended by a lady's maid. In respect of the master's suits and overcoats, the valet would usually have conferred with the nearest high class tailor, whereas the lady's maid usually made gowns, trimmed hats and arranged such adornments as ostrich feathers and beads so that each hat carried a noticeable style.

Each day she groomed Her Ladyship's hair using curling tongs heated by a spirit lamp to achieve the required style. She also helped Her Ladyship to dress and attended to such sundries as toilet cases, powders, perfumes and rouge. When the lady of the house went on a shopping spree to London or visited the family at another large house, the lady's maid usually accompanied her and the relationship was more like that experienced by sisters than employer and employee.

Beyond the main dining room several low ranking maids performed their duties which began each morning at five precisely. Their tasks were varied. Cleaning ashes from the fireplace and laying and lighting a fresh fire, ensuring that the outdoor valets had filled the scuttles with coal. Cleaning the hearth then polishing all the walnut and mahogany furniture with beeswax, sweeping the floors and carpets with a stiff broom before dusting around the many ornaments and potted palms. These tasks had to be completed by eight for at that hour the maids gathered in the main kitchen where each filled several copper cans with hot water. These they then carried up the stairs to each bedroom, knocked on the door and placed the can on the dresser while, at the same time, ensuring that the pot jugs were filled with clean cold water which, when the tenant of the bedroom had washed, they tipped into a bucket and struggled downstairs with it to the kitchen where it was swilled away.

Breakfast was served at eight thirty prompt and eaten in the dining room. The maids carried dishes of bacon, kidneys, eggs, porridge, kippers and tomatoes and placed them on the sideboard. Steaming hot pots of coffee and toast slices neatly arranged within silver racks were positioned upon the table.

When the family assembled, the maids and valets stood a little aside from them while the head of the household concluded morning prayers. When the family were seated and their needs being attended to, the butler, staff and maids went down to the kitchen for their own breakfast; then when all the dishes were cleaned they set about attending to their tasks according to the duty roster. There were beds to be made, hall-ways, staircases and carpets to be swept. Then, tables, chairs and bookcases to be dusted and polished.

They were allowed three meals a day and perhaps a small surreptitious supper around half past seven or eight in the evening. By nine, most of them had washed, slipped on a nightgown, taken a candle and climbed the stairs to her small room 'absolutely whacked' as one retired maid recently put it. This lady wishes to remain anonymous but, to retain some form of identity, I will call her Pat.

Just after her fourteenth birthday Pat was told by her father that she would be going into service, in fact her parents had already placed her on the books of a domestic services agency in Derby.

At that tender age she was not at all familiar with the term 'into service' until it was explained by her father, whereupon she burst into tears and standing before him retorted ''I'm not going skivvying for the rich folk''. But, in her own words, a 'skivvy' she became.

Pat received the news with anger, frustration and fear. ''I hated the thought of leaving my brothers and sisters. We were a close family, although there were eight or nine of us and I was the eldest. My goodness how I cried''.

But the day of her departure dawned and after hiring a pony and gig her father accompanied her to the railway station, bid her goodbye and added that he would be seeing her 'when she returned home for a long weekend in six months time'.

The salon. (Photograph: F.Parkes)

''For the first week I was in a state of nerves; especially when I saw the size of the house and all the well-to-do people connected with it. Mind you, the housekeeper was a lovely woman. She treated us all as daughters. ''Well, them upstairs are one family so we people downstairs will be another'' she used to say. And we were. In fact, after I got over the initial shock of leaving home I began to enjoy it.

But there were mornings – cold, frosty and foggy mornings – when I had to take a bucket, scrubbing brush and scraper and clean the stone steps leading up to the front door. It was so cold, it's a wonder the water didn't freeze the second I swished it over the stonework. And when I had done it, a footman used to come out and inspect the steps before I was allowed inside the house again. He might notice I'd missed a little patch of green moss and he'd stand over me until I'd scrubbed and scraped it away. "Right, I think that looks a bit better. I think you can go inside and report to the housekeeper again" he would say in a soft but stern voice. And I never saw him smile once that man. Never once.

Another person who'd stand over me while I was scrubbing was Her Ladyship. She'd stand there, hands clasped tightly behind her back and then when I'd finished she would say. "Now then young lady, do straighten your hat before you go back inside. And for goodness sake tuck your hair beneath it. In fact, you can tell the housekeeper that you've to get your hair cut and trimmed this very day."

But I never did. I had a lovely head of blonde curls and everybody used to remark upon the colour and texture of my hair so obviously it was the only thing I'd got to be proud of.

Now I look back I think Her Ladyship was jealous, or envious if there's any difference. Anyway, I never did get it cut. I'd go to the housekeeper and tell her what had been said then she'd stand with her hands on her wide hips, smile and say. "Well, just keep out of sight for a few days eh. I'll send somebody else out to scrub the steps tomorrow." But when everything seemed to have quietened and it was my turn to scrub the steps again, bless me if Her Ladyship didn't show up, ask me if I'd had my hair cut, tell me that it grew very quickly then step inside the door, turn and say. "Right, go straight to Mrs Gilbert and tell her to get the scissors on it, right now." But again, we never did!

When I got promoted, as they used to reckon I had been, my day still used to begin at five with cleaning the ash from the fireplaces in the main hall and dining room. Then I'd light the fresh fires and leave them only when flames were roaring up the chimney and the wood and coal was crackling like Billy-O.

Being still a low ranking maid, I had nothing to do with laying the table or serving the food so I used to go straight down to the kitchen, help with the frying and cooking then put the food on the plates for all the servant staff.

The amount put on each plate depended on your rank within the servant's hierarchy or matriarchy, whichever. For instance, the butler would qualify for three or four sausages whereas myself – the youngest and lowly one -might get half a sausage or even a whole one if I was lucky. If we were eating when the butler entered the servant's dining room we had all to stand until he was, seated.

Then we could sit down ourselves. When he rose – well we all had to stand again.

Some days they didn't need me to help with the washing up so I'd be detailed to dust the living room and salon. There the family portraits would be staring down at you as you moved the little clocks, ornaments and potted plants. Nor could you forget the wall ornaments like peacock feathers and antlers; mainly those of the Caribou, red and fallow deer stags. And the glass cases and domes containing stuffed birds, well they could prove a real headache. There didn't have to be so much as a single smear on those!''

The Great Hall. (Photograph: F.Parkes)

"Next job was to clean the carpets and, for that, several of us used to go down to the kitchen and come back carrying bowls filled with wet tea-leaves. These we used to spread across the carpet, let them soak in for about five minutes then sweep them on to a dustpan and the carpet had a sheen on it the likes of which I've never seen before or since, and I was a maid at thirteen other big houses after that first one.

On Wednesdays we'd finish at twelve, we youngsters. After our dinner I'd get changed then, if it was autumn or winter, I'd walk along the lime avenues and call at one of the gate-lodges. Here, after being invited in, I used to sit with the wife and we'd have a good old gossip and exchange a few household hints. Then about three we'd have a cup of tea in a china cup and a slice or two of seed cake. I'd visit a different lodge each Wednesday and sometimes there'd be another maid there and we'd have a right old discussion.

Annie lived in a gate-lodge just off the main road. She was a spinster, slender and grey haired. Her main job was to do the laundry for the gardeners who spent half a week in the bothies attached to the kitchen gardens. So she used to wash and scrub and cook for them – and their favourite dish believe it or not was sparrow pie. She achieved this by conferring with a keeper who merely scattered grain on a soil patch a few feet from her lodge, went inside with his shotgun and fired a single shot from the opened window when a flock of sparrows had flown in to feed.

Annie used to pluck, trim and cook all the little birds in a deep pie served hot with vegetables and gravy and the gardeners and propagating staff used to love it.

In the summer we were allowed out on the lake in a rowing boat. But we were always accompanied by a footman who did the rowing. He'd row quietly up to the coot families ferrying along by the water lily beds and scatter grain on the surface for them. This would also bring the swans across. It didn't matter if they were on the bank or in the water. They'd come over with their wings arched and six or seven cygnets paddling in file between them. The water lily beds were beautiful when they were in flower and there seemed to be more lilies in flower every year.

Some days Miss Gilbert, the housekeeper, used to let me take Her Ladyship's cairn terriers to the village post office where I'd collect His Lordship's mail. All the letters and documents used to be kept in a leather pouch with a lock zip at the top and golden insignia on the side.

Sundays, well we had no choice but to go to church. All of us. Miss Gilbert included. In the first years that I was employed at the Hall, his Lordship and Ladyship used to go in the coach in full regalia. Then they switched to a Rolls Royce. But, either way, we had to, walk. Even if it was raining. "That's what they've got umbrellas for," her Ladyship used to answer if we pointed out that it was pouring down and wondered if, just once, she might let us stay indoors.

In the church everybody had a special pew. We'd be at the back though. But there was no larking about I can tell you that. Some of the villagers used to be seated quite near to us and, my goodness, they knew everything that went off.

One Sunday morning, not long after I'd gone into service, one woman said to another just loud enough for me to hear. ''I see they've got a new skivvy up at the Hall''. Then all the heads of the people within earshot were turned towards me and they stared in a pitying sort of way, especially the women.

Well, as I said, we went home every six months. But not always at Christmas. In fact, very seldom at Christmas. But the estate people were always very good to our parents and every family was sent a hamper filled with peaches, pears and nectarines grown on the estate, plus a Christmas cake and haunch of lamb or venison.

But, in retrospect, I wouldn't go into service if I had my time to come over again. I mean, it was the nights used to upset me. Taking a candle up the stairs at nine and going into a room that you could just about get a single bed in, but with bars up at the windows. That was when I really used to start hankering after home.

And then when I think of myself scrubbing and scraping those stone steps with hands chapped so badly that you could have stood halfpennies up. in them. I again think, was it all worth it? Would I have expected my children to go into service? And the answer is – no, I definitely wouldn't.''

Awaiting his Lordship (Photograph: F.Parkes)

Although the last mentioned of the country house employees, the nanny was by no means the least important. In fact, she carried the same air of authority as the housekeeper and cook since it was her job to supervise the children of the house, until they were old enough to attend a boarding school. Nanny bathed and dressed the children and taught them table manners while her understudy, a nursery maid, made their beds, prepared clean clothes, warmed towels and collected water for their hot baths.

When Nanny took the children out, with the baby snuggled into a high wheeled black pram, the nursery maid cleared up their room and tidied the toys in the nursery.

After tea, the children were allowed to play longer, according to their age, before being bathed and settled into bed. Nanny's final task was to read them each a story and while this was taking place, their mother came up to the nursery and talked with them for a little while. Then the small assembly said their prayers. The children were tucked between the blankets and their mother, after kissing them, went quietly down the stairs while Nanny retired to her room by the nursery, for if there was a baby in the house, she had still to attend to its needs throughout the night and give a verbal report regarding its welfare, to Her Ladyship first thing in the morning.

SHERWOOD'S
ROYAL VISITORS

Whenever a member of the Royal Family visited Nottinghamshire, the villagers were seldom slow in celebrating such a memorable event. But there were several occasions when visits went unrecorded, particularly if one of the owners of the Dukeries estates was playing host to the Royal guests who had been invited to participate in the shooting parties that took place in the autumn and winter months. In the words of one elderly lady from Worksop:

"I was strolling along a ride in the Birklands with my husband and his parents one weekday afternoon, when a cavalcade of Rolls Royces suddenly appeared at the opposite end of the ride. It was obviously somebody of importance paying a visit and we all concluded that it must have been the Duke of Portland. Next thing, all the cars had parked and men wearing caps, bowler hats, tweed suits and plus fours were getting out and strolling down to one of the middle cars, presumably to get instruction from the Duke or his estate steward. As we got closer, I noticed one or two ladies among them and at least one had a little lap dog tucked beneath her arm. Some of the men nodded and touched their hats as we passed, then one, who had been standing with his back towards us, turned, smiled and wished a hearty, good morning to us and do you know it was our late King George VI. Now that walk in the Birklands, I'll never forget!''

Throughout the 1920s, King George V made a succession of visits to the Dukeries estates and no doubt invited his host's to the occasional shooting party held on the Royal Estate at Sandringham, North Norfolk.

A keen field-sportsman, King George V occasionally requested to view an estate's herd of red deer with the intention of shooting a particularly fine stag in mind. The target for all noblemen was a stag which in sporting terms was called a 'Royal'. This term immediately furnished the deer enthusiast with the awareness that the beast carried twelve evenly matching points, or tines, on his antlers. Each point or upright of an antler is given a name which links the present with mediaeval times and with the red deer in particular, the curved tines that rise above the forehead are called 'brow' tines. About four to six inches higher is a small tine, the 'bay or bez' tine. Higher up the main 'stem or beam' of the antler is the 'tray or trez' tine. Thus a Royal carried matching 'brow, bay and tray' tines and the division of tines at the top numbered three.

I should perhaps state here that a stag, carrying a similar formation on Exmoor or the Quantock Hills, was said to have been carrying all his 'rights' (brow, bay and tray tines) and three on each top.

Conversations, relating to sporting trophies and deer heads in particular, were commonplace at the Royal banqueting tables and one can imagine the dignitaries discussing antler formations after the meal when the men were gathered in the lounge or study, sipping from glasses of Port and smoking expensive cigars. The mounted head of an exceptionally fine 'Dukeries' stag, shot by the Duke of Portland in 1929 was donated to the Nottingham Natural History Museum and, in having viewed this specimen myself, I have taken note of the fact that the 'brow' tines are uneven. King George V undoubtedly commented on the stag heads displayed within the dining quarters of Welbeck Abbey or Thoresby Hall and if he chanced to select a Royal stag running with the Portland herd, he made no secret of the fact that he wanted to shoot it.

While the citizens of Nottingham may have been unaware that the owners of the Dukeries estates were due to receive Royal visitors, the people of Worksop and Mansfield were not because the visitors usually arrived by a special Royal train and had with them an entourage consisting of stewards, footmen, maids and butlers.

Having travelled north from Sandringham, King George V had acquired the habit of transporting his coach and horses by rail. The staff working at the railway stations must have seen the coachmen harnessing the team of splendid horses known as the 'Royal Windsor Greys', of which his Royal Highness was so fond. One can imagine the scene as the cavalcade of horses and coachmen left the station and took the road leading to Welbeck, Clumber or Thoresby. As prearranged the station-master telephoned the host's steward who in turn telephoned his employers at 'the big house'. They, in turn, informed their butlers and head housekeepers, who made ready for the occasion, and warned the servants to stay in their various stores and kitchens in readiness to be called upon. On a brisk autumn morning, the Royal Windsor Greys would have been a splendid sight as they trotted by the traces of golden foliaged woodland to the formal entrance of Welbeck Abbey.

The gatekeeper performed the task of opening the large gates by operating a series of mechanical gears, the moment he received word that the Royal procession was in sight. It was either himself or his wife, who telephoned the estate steward then sent word to the Duke of Portland or whoever was in residence at the time.

The main gates of Welbeck Abbey displayed pieces surmounted by lions, each holding a shield bearing the quarterings of the Duke and Duchess of Portland. Over each side of the gateways, shields carved into the stonework, bore the arms of the Cavendish and Bentick families respectively. Once inside the lodge gates, the Royal party had a three-mile journey along the formal tree-lined avenues before they reached the famed Welbeck Abbey.

On a mild October morning, the passengers in the coach might have seen a fallow buck parading around a herd of does and giving out his guttural call notes which informed both the members of the herd and rival bucks that he was in full rut and prepared to fight to retain his prime position.

Beneath the stands of oak and beech, groups of red deer hinds and their followers would have been feeding on calcium enriched acorns and beech mast, while a stag gave out his far carrying roars and scored the ground with down sweeping antlers.

His Royal Highness may have remarked upon the size of a particular stag and made further comments about the number of pheasants that proliferated the rides and parkland slopes. His coachmen may have enquired about the red bricked buildings, set back among the trees to the left and had been told that they represented St Cuthberts or Welbeck College.

Built in the domestic style of Queen Anne, the College contained a chapel founded by Lord Mountgarret 'a most generous friend to the school' and an assembly hall which was one hundred and thirty feet long and sixty-two feet high.

Thus, with the coach gently swaying and the arch necked Royal Greys snorting as they by-passed paddocks containing horses belonging to the Portland stables, the Royal party came within sight of Welbeck Abbey and the formal entrance, where the hosts and head servants were waiting to welcome them.

The rich aromatic scents of decaying leaves and beech mast may have infiltrated their nostrils when they were in the coach. But once inside the house these were exchanged for the taints of polish, venison roasts and later, port and cigar smoke. The shooting party was usually arranged for the following day and sometimes, between their arrival and the evening of their departure, his Royal Highness would have been given a tour of the Abbey, beginning with the underground rooms.

It was long rumoured that a member of the Cavendish-Bentick family, had spent two or three million having underground apartments constructed beneath the Abbey. Brick tunnels, people said, ran in every direction beneath the estate and some of the fifty lodge houses, used by their employees, were similarly constructed to give the occupants extra space. An anonymous visitor once wrote:

'The magnificent suite of rooms below Welbeck Abbey are lit by bulls-eye lamps from the roof above. Of these, the picture gallery is of the most startling dimensions and calculated to awaken the greatest interest. The walls of the corridors, by which it is approached, are decorated with works of art and would constitute a more ordinary collection. Mahogany fittings, tapestry hangings, portraits and decorations go to adorn the palace which geniuses have spent themselves in embellishing. The dimensions of the picture gallery are enormous when considering that it is all underground and lit from the roof. They are:

Length – one hundred and fifty eight feet
Width – sixty-three feet
Height – twenty-one feet

This vast area is illuminated by 1,100 burners and was originally intended for a ballroom. By the kindness of the Duke and Duchess, it was on occasions, thrown open for dances in aid of various charities. The wall's are studded with gems of the great masters. Here are examples of Sir Joshua Reynolds, Dr Mitters, Tintoretti, Barret, Bassano, De Voss Greffier, Van De Velde, Richardson, Wooton, Breughel, Van De Meulen, Vandyke, Holbein, Dali and others. A most notable and interesting picture of Welbeck, being that of the late Duke, the famous nobleman who made Welbeck one of the wonders of the world, will be seen at the end of the corridor as one is about to enter the great gallery. At one end of the gallery is a bust of the late Duke, the work of H R Pinker in 1880.'

The Welbeck estate catered admirably for its employees through the management of a social club, which contained a library, billiard room and refreshment lounge. Games of golf, cricket, bowls and football were encouraged by the Duke who was also an enthusiastic motorist.

Following a tour below ground, the Royal party would have perhaps been taken to the chapel, if they had not already visited it, in the company of the Duke's family who attended daily for the morning prayer meetings.

Called the new Welbeck chapel the architecture was an example of the classic style introduced by John of Padua and Havenius of Cleves. Further developments were carried out by Inigo Jones.

In general appearance, the chapel resembles some of the halls and chapels attached to the college of Oxford and Cambridge. It was actually planned by Mr John D Sedding who unfortunately died before the work was completed. His successor was Mr H Wilson who was entrusted with the responsible task of completing the work and designing the fittings.

The stone piers are placed in a Gothic edifice. The colours are warm brown and rest on bases of white marble with alabaster pedestals. The altar was designed by both Sedding and Wilson.

The riding school is situated some distance from the Abbey. It is connected by a subterranean passage, almost a mile long. I doubt that a visiting Monarch would have been guided along this route, although he may have been shown the entrance. Instead I suspect he was given a tour of the pleasure grounds and gardens before being shown into this building. Lit, at this time by eight thousand gas jets supported by fifty columns, the riding school dimensions were given as three hundred and eighty-five feet long, one hundred and four wide and fifty-one feet high. The riding school, built by the first Duke of Newcastle, displayed a clock in the roof turret. This was erected by a certain Mr Benson of Old Bond Street. It was for many years set to chime every quarter of an hour and, on the hour, a series of bells weighing twelve hundred weights came into play.

In an adjacent tower was a calendar which displayed separate indicators, the month of the year, the day of the month and the day of the week. Since December 1892, however, this building has been converted into a library and chapel.

Close to the riding school were the coach sheds, blacksmiths and farriers shop and both prize-winning horses and cattle were kept in the nearby enclosures.

With a great sense of pride, the head steward and his employer would guide the Royal party through the pleasure grounds, pointing out the Grotto archway, the rhododendrons valley and the avenues of yew, cedar and cypress trees.

In the formal gardens, they would view the sunken rose beds and the Rose Corridor which was one hundred and forty feet long. There was also a Camellia House, a Rosary and Palm House, an Apricot House and Peach House. A range of hot houses, divided into five sections, was devoted to the culture of pineapples, tomatoes and strawberries, while close at hand was the vinery where nectarines and muscatels were grown and harvested, alongside plums, figs, strawberries, peaches, pears and potted plants in the fruit house.

The tropical fruit house was used for the propagations of bananas, gooseberries, citrons and oranges. Finally, while touring the parklands in a coach or charabanc, the Royal guests would be taken to a block of newly erected houses known as the 'Winnings' which bore an inscription explaining their origin.

These houses were erected by the sixth Duke of Portland at the request of his wife for the benefit of the poor and to commemorate the success of his racehorses. In the years 1888, 1889, 1890 – Ayrshire, 2000 guineas and the

Derby, 1888; Donovan: the Derby and St, Ledger 1889, Memoir; The Oaks and St Ledger 1890, Semolina; One Thousand Guineas 1890.

The Winnings comprised of six houses, each of which had two bedrooms, a sitting room and kitchen. The residents were the Duke's oldest servants who were pensioned off, but never forgotten.

Before returning to the Abbey, the Royal coach would be driven along to Welbeck's famous Greendale Oak. Locally called 'the Methuselah of trees', the Oak was estimated to have been fifteen hundred years old, but I would think four or five hundred was closer to the mark. In 1724 an aperture was cut through the bole of the tree and sufficiently enlarged so that a carriage and four horses could be drawn through. Naturally this had a disastrous effect upon the tree's matured constitution and by the early twenties it was supporting but one bough of green foliage.

Major Rooke, a local naturalist and historian, measured the tree in 1779 and recorded its dimensions as:

Height of arch = Ten feet three inches
Width about the middle = Six feet three inches
Height of top branch = Fifty four feet

After having viewed this relic, I don't doubt that the conversation between the Royal visitors and Welbeck dignitaries returned to that of claret, cigars, pheasants and 'Royal' stags and a further account of days spent attending a shooting party will be given in the following chapter.

On the few occasions that a Royal party visited Clumber House, the coach journey from Worksop railway station, would have been a short but pleasant one, since the road led directly through the centre of Worksop via Park Street and out into the Sherwood Forest country by way of Spartan Hill.

Once through the lodge gates, the entourage would have probably remarked upon the splendour of the oaks, elms, limes and Scots pine trees, purple heather and thickets of golden flowering gorse.

One visiting scribe was immediately reminded of 'the forest which Shakespeare so well gives us a glimpse of in describing the scene in his play 'As You Like It'. Here and there in the park may be seen 'an old oak whose boughs were moss'd with age' and 'high top bald with dry antiquity'.

Besides mature trees, many newly planted trees were well established in Clumber Park by the turn of the century and in writing of this, an estate steward added that the intention was to keep up the pristine loveliness of the woodland glades, comprising of some four thousand acres and with its boundaries extending almost eleven miles, Clumber Park projected an atmosphere of wealth and tranquillity. In the woods on the Carburton side, the river Poulter had been fashioned into a great lake covering some eighty-seven acres and it goes without saying that several acres of landscape gardens, spanned the short distance between the French windows of Clumber House and the water's edge.

Clumber House, c. 1920. (Photograph: C.Shaw)

Standing by the chapel on a warm September morning, I watched a mute swan cob sailing arched winged over the lake and realised that many people in the past would have been similarly captivated by the whiteness of the bird progressing forcibly across the expanse of water reflecting the blue sky.

One can almost imagine King George V or the Prince of Wales studying the scene before it was suggested that they enter the formal porch of Clumber House which was built by the Duke of Newcastle in 1770.

Eventually, the house and estate passed through the marriage of the Duke's first granddaughter, Lady Margaret Cavendish – Harley, into the possession Portland family, but later reverted through further legacies to the Duke of Newcastle.

This family were patrons of the Arts, although some of the most valuable paintings were destroyed on March 26th 1879, when a fire swept through twenty rooms of the great house. The part of the house that was gutted by the fire was also the oldest part comprising of the West Front, Grand Staircase and Entrance Hall, but Mr Charles Parry, an eminent architect was asked to reconstruct that portion of the house and make it more palatial than that destroyed by the fire.

Clumber''s state dining room was sixty feet in length and thirty-four feet in width. It could satisfactorily accommodate one hundred and fifty guests.

The Royal visitors were shown paintings by Snyders, Langan, Weenix and Zuccarelli, then probably guided along the passage to the Grand Hall measuring eighty feet in length by forty-five feet in width. Here they would have seen a statue of Napoleon attributed to both Franzona and Canova, busts of Fox and Pitt by Nollekens, another bust by Belt, featuring the late Duke of Newcastle, and a bust of the fifth Duke by Dewick who lived in the nearby town of Retford. Also prominently displayed was a Gainsborough depicting a forest scene.

The grand staircase was engraved from marble. When the Prince of Wales paid a visit in 1868, the Grand Drawing Room had just been decorated and he regarded it as one of the most interesting apartments within the mansion.

Here were hung paintings by Vandyke, Murillo, Castiglioni and Lawrence, alongside ornaments from the Doges Palace Venice and the King's Palace Bermuda. The Prince of Wales and other Royal guests were particularly impressed by the library with its fittings of Spanish mahogany and handsome tables and cabinets made from walnut and rosewood.

The study contained an elaborate marble chimney brought for fifteen hundred pounds from a sale at Fonthill Abbey. Besides family portraits, Gainsboroughs, Holbeins and Rubens, the room took one back to the Civil War by displaying portraits of Charles I and II.

The billiard room was recorded as being 'a pleasant retreat in which this popular game may be indulged.'

Following their sumptuous dinners, the Royal guests and their hosts probably strolled for a quarter of a mile along the margins of the lake for here, at a cost of seven thousand pounds, the pleasure gardens had been tastefully designed to include marble statues and sculptured vases, while anchored alongside was 'The Lincoln' a pleasure boat, then described as a vessel estimated to have weighed forty tons.

A visit to Clumber church which is situated close to the Ducal mansion was a foregone conclusion and prayer meetings were conducted here for the Royal guests. The choir comprised mainly of boys from Clumber Hostel which was financially maintained by the Duke of Newcastle and 10031 historians were never slow in illustrating the fact that both the hostel and church were among the Duke's earliest considerations when he came into possession of the 'great estate'

Building began in 1886 and the place of worship was opened on 23rd October 1889 with the Bishops of Lincoln and Southwell taking part in the elaborate ceremony. The architects were Bodley and Garner, both of which suggested a pure Gothic style to which the Duke readily agreed. The imposing spire is one hundred and eighty feet high. It contains but a single bell that weighs about thirty-three hundredweights.

Before leaving Clumber, a visiting monarch would have no doubt ridden one of the Duke's horses and visited his kennels, housing pointers, labradors, setters and spaniels, all of which were trained for marking down and retrieving ground game.

The same kennels would have contained the dog breed which took its name from the estate 'the Clumber Spaniel'. The origin of this breed has constantly puzzled the canine experts, who in speculation have linked the Basset hound, the Alpine and Brittany spaniels, although in some ways the Clumber resembles a stocky pale coated strain of Newfoundland. However its pedigree as such has never been disclosed and, while the breed is certainly acceptable for its values (domestic), I suspect that it was not popular with both the shooting fraternity and huntsmen since it was mute and thereby failed to advertise the location or direction of its quarry.

While touring the Dukeries, the Royal party would also have visited Thoresby Hall, which was then owned by the Manvers family. A steward would have recommended that the distinguished guests travel by way of the Classical Bridge spanning the river Poulter near Carburton, then passed alone the tree-lined avenue to the lodge gates on the Thoresby border. Here some now forgotten gentleman recorded that 'the visitors emerged into the park with the deer bounding and starting at his footfall'.

Thoresby Park is over twelve miles in circumference with its north easterly tracts covered by heather, gorse and beech forests. The eastern slopes are crowned by a fine wood of pines and various firs, while to the south and south east, the foliage line changes in shape, for this side of the park lands were planted with oaks, sweet chestnuts and lime that have long matured and created both an excellent habit for wildlife and the atmosphere of seclusion that was desired by the planners of bygone times.

The lake, created by the inflow of the river Meden, enhanced a long valley to the west and is still considered to be the finest stretch of water in Nottinghamshire. Reedy and fringed by alder and silver birch, the lake provides habitat for many species of wintering ducks.

Thoresby Hall. (Photograph: C.Shaw)

Close to the house, gardens were created and terraces, at the rear of which stood the estate workshops. The original Thoresby Hail was built of brick. The mansion that we see today however was built of Steetly Stone and the building operations carried out by a highly recommended firm based In London. The architect was a Mr A Salvin.

Once between Thoresby's massive iron gates, King George V may have remarked upon the encaustic tiles which were transported from Germany. Weapons of war, sporting guns and the mounted heads of stag, fox and otter adorned the walls of the entrance hall. Two flights of steps, tightly fitted with red carpet, took the Royal visitor to the Grand Hall with its floor of Sherwood Forest oak skilfully laid into an appropriate pattern with a parqueterice border.

A Steetly Stone chimney supported by columns of granite was probably the most interesting feature of the hall because it was surrounded by a colossal representation of the host's entire family carved in stone. Two fine busts of the Ducs De Ciogny, ancestors of the Dowager Countess Manvers, with many other family portraits and costly relics adorned the Grand Hall.

The Grand Staircase, with its steep stone steps hewn from Roche Abbey, led to a handsome gallery from which the upper apartments of the house extended.

The dining room was forty feet long, twenty-six feet wide and twenty feet high. The ceiling was decorated with geometric figures; the walls panelled with walnut. Family portraits were displayed alongside paintings by Creswick, Andsel, Vicat Cole and Melbey.

The small drawing room, with its deep red satin damask hangings, contained portraits of the Earl and Countess Manvers, who were the owners in the early to mid-1920s. The library, panelled with forest oak, boosted another magnificent chimney piece with an elaborately carved Sherwood Forest scene said to have been taken from the Birklands. It depicts a cluster of venerable Sherwood oaks and a herd of deer exquisitely carved by a Mr Robinson of Newark. Statues of Robin Hood and Little John supported each side of the piece which was nearly fifteen feet high and ten feet wide.

Of all the state apartments, the grand drawing room was perhaps the most elaborate with solid fittings consisting of maple, walnut and oak. The marble pieces were fashioned from blocks of snow white marble bearing ornamental designs representing the four seasons. Extending some fifty-three feet in length and twenty-five feet in width, the walls were covered with damasks of blue satin.

Pink, blue and gold were blended into the ceiling decorations, while the rich upholstery of the carved and gilded furniture finalised the effects of other luxuries, just as the owners and designers intended. The most prized possession in the room was a handsome vase mounted on a pedestal 'by the Empress Eugene to the Countess Manvers in 1854'.

The house also includes a fine billiard room and no less than sixty bedrooms, most of which had dressing rooms attached.

Before leaving Thoresby I don't doubt the visiting Monarch was led across an extremely pretty bridge crossing the Meden. One such visitor touring the house and grounds in the late summer recorded the bridge as completely 'embosomed in the most luxuriant foliage. Indeed such sylvan profusion is rarely to be met with'.

It is also worth recording that when they eventually left the Sherwood Forest country, the visiting Monarchs continued to enthuse upon the splendours of each great house and the hospitality extended by the owners.

King George V also spoke of having seen Sherwood Forest's occasional Royal stag when waiting for the pheasants to rise before his gun barrel.

HOSTS OF THE PRINCE OF WALES

"There never came a maid to the greenwood tree who failed to pay the forester's bounty fee". One Royal visitor to whom these words of local folk lore were said to have appealed was the Prince of Wales who was entertained at Rufford Abbey in 1888.

Situated two miles from Edwinstowe, Rufford Abbey was founded by the Earl of Lincoln in 1148. Here a society of Cistercian or White Monks from Rivaulx Abbey Yorkshire, became quickly established until the reign of Henry VIII, when during the dissolution of such monasteries, there were fifteen cannons inhabiting the Abbey and receiving an annual revenue of one hundred and seventy six pounds, and twelve shillings and sixpence from the state. Few traces of the ancient Abbey exist but the servants' hall that we see today is thought to have been the monks' refectory.

Before he retired in 1888, the owner Baron Savile was a distinguished member of the diplomatic service, and during his career represented Britain at various congressional meetings held in Europe and America.

He acquired the title of Lord Savile on the death of his brother,

Mr Augustus Savile, in April 1887 and during his tenure of the estate, carried out improvements and a refurbishing programme which included the complete renovation of the Picture Gallery.

Thus he would have been eager to have shown his guest the Prince of Wales the Grand Staircase and new east wing, lit when required, by the recent installation of electric lighting which served the entire premises along with a new and much improved water scheme.

Being an artist himself he would have lost no time in showing the Prince his collection of paintings, while reminding his Royal guest that when he was at Petersburg in 1864 – 1865, he was elected as an Associate of the Imperial Russian Academy of Antwerp. Displayed at Rufford were paintings by Vandyke, De Hasse, Hildebrant, Leon Herbo, Rembrandt and Severdonck, as well as Lord Savile's own personal works which included his first canvas 'Interior of a

Highland Bothy'. There was also a gallery of family portraits by Sir Peter Lely, Sir Joseph Reynolds, Vandyke, Romney and Kneller. Lord Savile also presented to the nation over one hundred valuable paintings which were hung in the National Gallery. Among them were works-by Velasquel, Murillo, Chardin and Steenwick.

Lord Savile died in November 1896 and was succeeded by his nephew who, once his accession to the title and estate had been established, strove to maintain the high standards and best traditions of his uncle.

During his term of ownership, King Edward VII visited Rufford Abbey quite frequently and it was no doubt mentioned that James I, his son Charles, and George IV, also stayed there. Another famous guest was Dibdin, who was said to have composed his song 'Woodman, spare that tree' after returning from a walk in the nearby forest.

Edward VIII also visited Rufford on the few memorable occasions he came to Nottinghamshire. Known affectionately to many of the locals as 'our Teddy', Prince Edward became the Prince of Wales and, after serving in the naval training establishment, took a commission in the Grenadier Guards.

He excelled at golf and tennis throughout his years as a young man and enjoyed field sports, particularly rough shooting which involved walking the fields and coverts with spaniels and retrievers at the heel, and ready to retrieve the pheasants, partridges and hares when they were shot.

Being a blond handsome man, Edward was sometimes called Prince Charming by many of the peers, their families and particularly their daughters. Retired servant staff who had worked at some of the five houses in 'The Dukeries' told me that there was a noticeable atmosphere of discreet romanticism in the air whenever the Prince was making a visit and Rufford was the house at which he particularly enjoyed staying.

A meeting with a retired builder's labourer who had worked on most of the most exclusive properties in north Nottinghamshire furnished me with the following observations.

"There was a great sense of excitement generated throughout the district whenever the Prince of Wales was staying at Rufford or visiting Welbeck and Thoresby.

I remember my father and myself re-settling some tiles on a roof section at Rufford. I was up the ladder and my father was working below, when the head gardener and the estate steward approached him in a very serious manner. After talking in low voices the two men walked down the path and my dad shouted up to tell me to finish off what I was doing then come down.

It appeared that the Prince of Wales was due in that afternoon and Lord Savile had given instructions that none of the servant staff, gardeners or builders must be seen about the place.

This of course included the laundry-maids and any of the everyday workfolk connected with the smooth running of the great house. So we went home and returned the next day after a dance had been held in the Prince's honour.

My word! To eyes unaccustomed to seeing such sights it was like *Alice in Wonderland.* There were coaches, carriages and charabancs parked alongside the gravel drives and people strolling about the gardens in splendid jackets and top hats.

When I told the head footman that I didn't recognise many of the people present, he replied to the effect that he didn't expect I would because although some were part of the Royal entourage others had travelled the relatively short distances from Welbeck, Thoresby, Clumber and Worksop Manor, each as part of a separate entourage, because when titled folk travelled in those days they took their servant staff with them. The head footman then told me about the dances which were held in the Prince's honour. Bejewelled ladies wearing the latest creations from London and Paris. Handsome men eager to be admired as they strutted around in their tuxedos.

Hired musicians came in charabancs and rickety taxis. Some local men were among them, others were summoned from London with rail ticket and hotel bill paid in advance. All the families of the Dukeries great houses were present. They were driven along the grand avenues in Daimlers and Rolls Royces. Not just one or two cars but a whole fleet of them.

You can hardly imagine it to-day. But it happened all right. Two or three times a year, or whenever Royalty chose to stay over for a few days.

The day following an evening of drinking and dancing was usually the one in which the Royal guests quietly toured the glades of Sherwood Forest. Especially the Prince of Wales who was 'occasionally driven in a Daimler with startling white wheels'.

Two of the venue's listed for the Prince's attention were Edwinstowe, legendary home of Robin Hood and Maid Marion, and the Major Oak. One steward-guide began some notes, destined for the Prince's ear, with the following words:

'We are now about to plunge into the very heart of the ancient forest where the splendid oaks and the deer boundary fence in the distance indicate that few changes have taken place for centuries in this charming region.' He was writing of Bilhagh, which along with the other houses in the district, was once a Royal park enclosed and holding herds of red and fallow deer. Bilhagh was originally granted to the Duke of Portland by the Crown, but over several generations, the Duke exchanged it in order to acquire 'other properties' then owned by the Manvers family. Just before the Prince of Wales was driven into Edwinstowe village his chauffeur would have been quietly directed to the right and along a green ride where the famous Major Oak then lived up to its reputation as 'the mighty giant of the forest'. Major Rooke had recorded the fact that the trunk of this much-visited oak, measured thirty-two feet in circumference around the roots, thirty feet around the base at the height of five feet and a circumference covered by the boughs of two hundred and forty feet.

Prince Edward posing beside his chauffeur-driven Daimler. (Photograph: C.Shaw)

The root system was spread for some ninety feet around this and the nearby silver birch trees and the famed hollow in which legend insists Robin Hood once hid, was seven feet in diameter and fifteen feet in height.

Two miles from Edwinstowe, on farmland owned by the Duke of Portland Street and the ruins of King John's Hunting Palace. Because the ruins were of such great historic interest the Prince of Wales included them in at least one of his tours of the Nottinghamshire Dukeries and also included the famous Parliament Oak, within his itinerary.

It is believed that in 1212, King John, who was out hunting in the forest received news, via a courier, of a revolt in Wales and summoned the barons to attend a meeting beneath this tree to decide what measures to take to repress the Celtic threat.

Edward I, also held a Parliamentary meeting nearby, though some authorities say that it probably took place in the hunting palace at Clipstone, rather than beneath the boughs of the already established Parliament Oak. Perhaps I should mention here that when the Prince of Wales was visiting the forest, coal mining was a flourishing industry in the Clipstone area and while on his travels the Prince would undoubtedly have glimpsed the pitheads rising above the trees.

On the drive from Edwinstowe to Welbeck the Royal party may have pulled in at Clipstone Lodge which spans the centre of a grassy ride. Built in 1842, the Lodge was fittingly designed with Gothic patternings from an earlier design that can be seen today on the gate house at Worksop Priory. Known locally as 'the Duke's archway' the lodge is interesting from the viewpoint of there being figures of Robin Hood, Maid Marion, Little John, Richard Coeur de Lion, Friar Tuck and Alan-a-Dale displayed in the alcoves and niches of its ornate exterior. Finally the Royal tour usually included visits to two further trees, a then gigantic specimen known as the 'Simon Forester Oak' and the Butchers Shambles Oak, which the residents of nearby Edwinstowe village, frequently called 'Robin Hood's Larder'.

Having completed his tour of the Robin Hood country the Prince of Wales would probably be thinking of the following day's shooting party and its hosts and guests whom he might meet on the route to Welbeck or Rufford. And after the days sport there would be more formal dinners and dances held in his honour and hosted as one steward wrote 'in the best Dukeries tradition'.

The day before a shooting party was due to take place, the estate steward would have conferred with the head gamekeeper who in turn called upon each of the under-keepers with his instructions. Wives and laundry-maids would be busy ironing trousers, checking jackets and ensuring that a clean shirt and detachable collar, complete with shining stud, was hung on a coat hanger and placed in the man's wardrobe. Nor was footwear overlooked. Boots were polished 'so that you could see your face in em'. Gaiters and spats were checked for fraying edges. Everyone was expected to look immaculate, as indeed they did by the time the day eventually dawned.

Meanwhile in the stewards' office, the headkeeper would list the estate coverts that he thought ought to be drawn in respect of the number of pheasants they harboured. He would then visit the gunroom and probably confer with his underkeeper there or around the kennels where the spaniels, setters and retrievers were housed.

Guns would be cleaned and cartridges checked, then and a little later in the day each of the beaters would be called upon and given the time and place at which they should meet.

One retired, Nottinghamshire gamekeeper told me that 'the headkeeper was always on edge several days before a shoot took place because the gentry were looking to him to produce a good show of pheasants.

"And we lesser mortals of the English country estate never earned praise from anyone. By that I should perhaps explain that if the previous summer had been hot and dry, the hundreds of pheasant chicks that we had hatched under broody hens survived to adulthood. Consequently they were to be seen everywhere about the estate.

But if it happened to have been a wet summer the mites died of chill or pneumonia through searching for food in the soaking grasses. Being so young they had no resistance to chill because they were just balls of fluff about twice the size of a bumble bee.

"But whether if had been a good pheasant year or not, the visiting gentry were always invited along for a day's sport, and if there was a good crop of pheasants they used to emphasise that it was due to the past summer having produced the right conditions for rearing the chicks. But if there was a poor show of birds along the rides and in the coverts it was the gamekeeper's fault. Whatever has the man been doing over the past two seasons? Is he an alcoholic or something?"

Besides checking that the guns were clean the head gamekeeper and his underkeepers conferred about which of the several game carts they were going to use for carting the dead birds home the following day, while the steward made arrangements with the head footman or coachman to have the shooting brake waiting and ready to transport the most important guests from the parklands to the palatial mansion once the shoot was over.

Gamecarts covered a variety of designs and usually had raised sides for the day's tally or 'bag' was generally estimated to be a large one. It was not unusual for the guns' to account for six or seven hundred pheasants in a single day, particularly when the previous summer had yielded a good breeding season. The shooting brake had a raised seat at the front on which sat the driver and a companion, and in the middle were seats allowing six people to sit facing one another.

King George V, the Prince of Wales or any of the visiting nobility would have been conveyed in this vehicle. But the ladies, both guests and hosts, also travelled the short way with them back to the house, unless of course, a second shooting brake had been laid on. When the day of the shoot dawned all the gamekeepers, coachmen, estate blacksmiths, and farrier would be about the outbuildings. While the family and their guests were having breakfast, then attending prayers, usually taken in the morning room, the beaters would cycle in from the village and join the gardening and propagating staff, some of whom were also engaged as beaters.

An underkeeper usually met these gentlemen at the door of the gunroom, and each beater was given a pale overall which he wore over his rough suit.

The headkeeper's task was to ensure that the guns, ammunition and gundogs were ready, and after he had sent messages to the coachmen and stable boys, an older more responsible team of men would report to him as detailed by the estate steward. Their task was to carry the guns and ammunition as well as load and unload the guns of the gentry as they were needed. Out in the parklands an underkeeper checked the edges of the woods and coverts that were to provide the day's sport. When he discovered many pheasants feeding on the acorns and beech-nuts around the periphery of the trees, he would gently walk them back to the rhododendron coverts and have an old dog trotting fox-like ahead of him.

Rhododendrons and bamboo, incidentally, were planted specifically for the use as pheasant covert when field sports really came into their own midway through the eighteenth century. Bamboo was also used to screen the tunnels used by the duck decoymen who reared mallards for the shoot in the same way as the gamekeepers reared the estate pheasants.

When the guests appeared at the formal entrance of the great house, it was usually to remark upon the peacock which had been surreptitiously driven up to the entrance lawns, by a boy, a few minutes beforehand.

Then the shooting brakes, drawn by a couple of sturdy old horses, would transport the guests to the edge of the woods and coverts intended to be 'driven' that day and here they would meet the head gamekeeper, underkeeper and gun loaders, each of which was assigned to the aid of one particular person.

I don't doubt that a pecking order existed even among the gun loading fraternity, and it would not be unreasonable to suggest that the head game-keeper's eldest son, catered for a Royal guest alongside a son of the estate steward.

One can imagine the men and women arriving at their pegs and sitting on their shooting sticks, the gun handlers standing alongside and admiring the various makes of gun, especially those crafted by Mr Henry Holland of Bond Street.

For a time, the shooters would relax. The women in their cocked or feathered hats, two piece suits with jackets and long skirts, and black boots peeping from the hems of their skirts, when they sat upon the shooting sticks. Neatly manicured hands shielded by expensive gloves.

The men would be wearing caps and trilbies, neat shirts, ties or cravats, three quarter length coats, hard wearing trousers and plus fours. One or two might have quietly smoked a cigar or pipe, while they stood quietly conferring with gun handlers and remarking upon the weather, the season, their latest angling forays and the abundance or scarcity of local hares and pheasants. A short distance from the shooters, the dog handlers would be stationed and gently cajoling with the retrievers and spaniels. The beaters entering the far side of the wood, may have seen the game-keepers gibbet, his hanging post, where the rotting bodies of stoats, weasels, hedgehogs, carrion crows, jays, magpies, tawny, barn and little owls, sparrow-hawks and kestrels were displayed.

A full gibbet was an indication that the gamekeeper was doing his job. The same could be said of the string of mole corpses strung along the strand of wire placed above the post and rail fence, for quite a number of estates were still affluent enough to have employed at least one mole catcher, and perhaps several warreners, who along with the gamekeeper and his underkeepers, spent his days digging out rabbits aided by a ferret and a stock of purse and long nets; or walking the rough tracts of parkland, and shooting the many rabbits he saw feeding among the grasses and clover.

Among the shooters listening to the beaters attempting to ˙put up the pheasants was the sporting parson and perhaps an eminent local doctor or surgeon. Although men of the medical profession were often invited to join the 'steward's day' on the estate.

As its name implies, this was a day's shooting reserved for those being in the privileged position of estate stewards or land-agents. Their guests numbered stewards from the neighbouring country estates, the sporting parsons, gentlemen farmers and, as I've mentioned already, members of the medical profession, joined perhaps by a local magistrate or two.

Eventually the shooting party waiting at their pegs, would see beaters coming through the woods, tapping the tree trunks, whistling or calling out 'away yer go then'.

Blackbirds and flocks of finches would fly well below the tree-line when they were disturbed, but the shooters always hoped that the pheasants would fly high when eventually, they took to the wing.

Suddenly pheasants in their dozen would be cannonading out of the woods and the gun bearers handed out to each member of the shooting party their loaded guns.

'Here we go. Straight overhead. One to your left. Another coming over right. Good shooting sir!'

The scene is now one of pheasants flying above the guns, the shooters swivelling and leaning forward before firing. The shots resounding through the woods and across the parklands.

Some men shot wide and quietly cursed their predicament. Others displayed combinations of accuracy and speed. The results were pheasants plummeting from the sky, making colourful mounds upon the grass while the dogs strained to be unleashed. Another fusillade of shots and then the cry from the estate steward or head gamekeeper 'All out and all over'. The beaters then emerged from the wood. The dog handlers released their charges. The estate owner, who was usually known as his Lordship, conferred with the steward and the head gamekeeper about the next belts of woodland to be drawn.

Encouraged by their handlers the spaniels and retrievers would quickly retrieve the fallen birds, while the game cart, drawn by a fine old horse, was brought alongside the bank or edge of a path. Here the dead birds were laid out brace by brace. Mostly pheasants, but with the occasional partridge or wood-cock amongst them. The Royal guests and their hosts, including the ladies present, always made a point of inspecting the dead game birds, and when this was done the underkeepers counted them, bird by bird, then entered the tally into a notebook. Quite often these underkeepers were joined by the head gamekeeper, who was never very far from the proceedings, having earlier informed the beaters, dog handlers and gun loaders of the next area selected for a further round of sport.

While the hosts and guests were mingling, the handlers, beaters and loaders made their way across the parkland, mostly on foot, although occasionally a cart or carriage may have been laid on so that the gentry would not be kept waiting for too long.

Two further conveyances were then drawn alongside the shooting party. The first being the shooting brake in which the host and his Royal guest stood by to allow their ladies to be seated first and then chose seats close together so that they could continue their conversations while enjoying a cigar, or partaking from the contents of a hip flask.

When the shooting brake was driven away, the underkeepers loaded the dead game into the game cart, then turned the horses in the direction of the next wood to be shot over. Sturdy, cross-bred horses were preferred for the task of dray and cart pulling, and one can imagine the low flushes of winter sunlight highlighting their trappings, harness, brasses and heavy collars, as the group moved away.

The shooting party usually visited two or three of the estate woods and coverts before retiring around mid-day, when they would return to the country seat for lunch, while the rest of the estate staff made their bay to the various workrooms where the guns were cleaned, the dogs fed and watered and clothes changed and hung in personal lockers. The gamekeeper made a tally of all the game shot and it was not unusual for six or seven hundred pheasants to be listed alongside a few hares, partridges, woodcock and mallard, which was then simply referred to as a wild duck.

At some chosen hour in his week the host would enter the figures of shot game into a beautifully bound and embossed Game Book, that was usually given a place of honour on one of the bookcase shelves in his private study or library.

Occasionally, I have been granted the privilege of seeing several estate Game books and can vouch for the fact that the writing in each was neat and legible, and the tally entered with one figure set immediately beneath the next.

On some pages, the listings were accompanied by such comments as 'We found ourselves in the throes of a surprisingly early blizzard' or 'Her Ladyship did not attend this outing, having confined herself to the house in an attempt to overcome a heavy cold'.

There was, of course, always a reference to a Royal guest having attended a shoot. 'It gave us great pleasure this weekend, to be hosting the Prince of Wales, for whom the pheasants flew high and therefore provided His Royal Highness with much pleasant sport'.

One of the Prince of Wales' favourite tracts of Nottinghamshire woodland was *The Birklands*; perhaps originally called The Birchlands because silver birch proliferate there. However, it was once very much an area hidden by the crowns of some sizeable oaks. The Birklands are best viewed today, by walking the green ride which extends for some five miles throughout the woodland.

For the bird-watcher, all three species of woodpecker, tree-creeper and nuthatch breed here. The occasional sparrow-hawk may be glimpsed pursuing a flock of finches through the glades, and the summer visiting warblers, spotted flycatchers and redstarts, thrive within this rich and varied habitat.

In the Prince of Wales' day however, a Russian log hut was maintained close to the marshy tract, and used as a shooting lodge. Here the members of the shooting party could change into fresh socks or plus fours if they became wet or muddy. Trilbys, caps and jackets were also stored in the lockers along with bottles of brandy, port and whisky and as one elderly gamekeeper explained to me with a wink "a good time was usually had by all".

There are also several sites in the Dukeries where these shooting lodges were built. Some were used in the same way as a bird-watchers hide, but any mallard or teal which came down to the water were quickly shot rather than viewed through binoculars.

Because yew trees have a reputation for quick growth and provide satisfactory screening, it became fashionable to plant stands of yew on the woodland side of the shooting huts, and by locating these yew stands the late Eric Spafford and myself were able to draw up a short list of the small pools in the Dukeries alongside which shooting lodges had been erected and later disbanded.

One such site has now been encompassed by the Nottingham City boundary, but it 'can still be discerned as one walks the path around the Wollaton Park lake. On the west side of the lake, Thompsons Wood narrows into a swampy tract beyond which stands the boundary wall and the houses of Wollaton Vale. If a walker pauses by the fence and looks at the overgrown channels below, he or she will perhaps be surprised to learn that this site was originally dug out and maintained as a sizeable duck decoy for the Middleton estate.

Several pools still shimmer beneath the hedges, reeds and bracken, as the small aquatic zone widens and then terminates by a raised bank where the woodland suggests a firmer footage on dry land. There among the sycamores and black poplars, a fringe of yew trees can be seen to this day, thereby commemorating the fact that the estate gamekeepers and duck decoy man of seventy or eighty years ago, regularly visited and stocked up the lockers of the shooting lodge that was built there.

Besides visiting the Dukeries the Prince of Wales also toured the estates south of the forest and in all probability, visited the Manvers family residence at Holme Pierrepont Hall.'

I often wonder if he also shot wildfowl on the once lonely and lovely stretch of flood plain then known as Lenton Marshes. This natural sanctuary for wildfowl and waders extended across the flooded fields, that lay between the banks of the Trent opposite Clifton Grove and the hedgerow bordering the towpath section of the Nottingham canal. Today, what little remains of the fields are screened by an industrial estate of which the Players Horizon factory is best known among the many modern glass-fronted buildings.

Fortunately however, a farmhouse still stands besides the river a short distance from the industrial estate's boundary. Perhaps not surprisingly, this house is known as Trentside Farm, but in my mother's day almost everyone in Nottingham referred to it as 'The Prince of Wales Farm' because this eminent gentleman was said to have stayed there on several occasions, and at dusk rowed across the river to visit a certain lady who was residing at Clifton Hall.

END OF AN ERA

Throughout the 1920s, many of the village sages predicted that within a further decade the 'world of 'the owd horse and cart', as they put it, would be a thing of the past. Nor were these predictions without foundation for the canal barges and long boats were already facing redundancy due to the cheaper and faster rates offered by the railway haulage companies.

To add further injury to that of the changing world was the popularity of the Fordson tractor which first appeared on the agricultural scene in 1917.

Described by the Government of that time as being 'wholly reliable, sturdy and efficient', the Fordson company secured an order for six thousand tractors and other such implements to help the food production campaign established during the First World War

The Government's order arrived at the Fordson headquarters a little late in respect of them being able to produce that number of tractors. But however many they produced were greatly accepted by the agricultural communities and after the war the Fordson was deemed a great success and regarded as being the most popular tractor in British farming.

Lawrence Baker, who was a boy at that time living at the cottage in Shepherds Wood, recalls his father and grandfather standing beside their shoe repairs shed and saying. "Aye, that's the end of the plough and its team as we've known it. They'll be replacing the horse and cart with flat-backed lorries next. And the seed drill – that'll be mechanised before yer know it."

Within a matter of years there were teams of horses pulling the plough on one farm and a Fordson tractor being driven and cutting furrows at the next. And along the roads and lanes horse drawn carts and the pony and traps were occasionally overtaken by a flat backed lorry which in Nottinghamshire first won popularity with the coal delivery merchants. Lionel Baker, about whom you have read in the first two chapters has long nurtured an anecdote connected with these times and chuckles quietly as he relates the story of a Wollaton man who was employed as drayman by one such merchant.

"Everyday, no matter where he was, this drayman made sure that he was pulling his horse and cart up alongside the Admiral Rodney pub in Wollaton village at twelve noon on the dot. Everyday that is except for Sunday when the pub was closed and the man wasn't working anyway.

The horse got so used to this routine that it needed no second bidding and all the drayman had to do was spring off his dray onto the pavement and in the door of the Admiral Rodney taproom. There was never any need for him to put the brakes on because the horse pulled up as a matter of course.

Then, one week, the drayman bounced into the taproom with the news that his employer was 'going motorised'. By that he meant that the horse was going out to grass; retirement and the drayman was to become the driver of a flat backed lorry.

Well, on the last Friday dinner all the Rodney's locals stood outside the pub patting the horse and feeding him sugar lumps. Then, on the Monday at twelve noon, the drayman drove up in this noisy lorry, edged it into the kerb, leaped from the cab and entered the taproom.

"So you've come in your lorry today then," his drinking companions murmured rhetorically. Then one of them said: "Did you put the brake on?"

"Put the brake . . . ? Christ! No, I didn't!".

Slamming his pint class on the bar the drayman ran outside, followed by his companions, in time to see the lorry coasting steadily down Church Hill. Suddenly the drayman broke into a run, shaking his fists and yelling. "Hey! Stop! Whoa, yer bugger, Whoa!" But the vehicle stopped only after it had dismantled a horse trough situated beside the Rectory hedge on the tight curve of road beside the Wollaton Park wall."

Needless to say, the horse trough was never rebuilt because anyone credited with half a grain of foresight could see that the horse and dray were to be replaced by lorries and haulage waggons of all shapes and sizes.

By the time I was born in 1938 the canals had fallen into a full state of redundancy and the railway marshalling yards were busy with men loading and off-loading freight from the waggons, of what were then known as 'the goods trains'; 'goods' being an alternative term for merchandise.

There were still several carters employed by the tobacco manufacturers, John Player and Sons Ltd, and the carters' café that Lionel Baker had known was well patronised until the beginning of the 1950s.

By the time I could walk a fair distance however, cars and lorries were being driven along the ring roads. Not in any great numbers, but they were there nonetheless.

It was on the Sunday morning walks around Wollaton and Strelley with my father, that I began noticing the artefacts which signified the closing scenes to times gone by. They stood out like exhibits in a museum, which in some ways I suppose they were. Exhibits displayed in the Museum of Life.

At Browns Woodyard I walked with Dad by deserted cart sheds but with the carts and drays still parked there. Brightly painted, dark blue, dark red and forgotten. On the opposite side of the lane stood the blacksmith and farrier's forge; empty. Alongside them an extended stable block housed only breeding colonies of rats and mice which were preyed upon by the pair of barn owls, who still reared an annual brood in the old rafters and refused to leave.

Woodyard Lane, Wollaton, the main thoroughfare to Brown's Sawmills

At Balloon crossroads I loved the deep foliaged silence of the woods and wandered the glades and explored the sand-pits uninterrupted, and with Granny Simmonds dead some twenty years since.

On the opposite bank of the canal at Radford Woodhouse a grey barge was moored beside a derelict boat repairer's cabin. The foreman's home, Pear Tree Cottage, was still intact and is being lived in to this day.

Higher along the canal, on its winding route towards the Derbyshire border, two larger barges, with bases overgrown by reed and giant waterdock, provided sanctuary for the moorhens which ferried between these and the bramble-overhung banks. Either side of the barges stood other remnants of the past. One being a railway cabin, its doorway framed by pink and red roses. This had been the home of the canal lengthman, Percy Ping and his wife who lived there until ill health forced them to move into an old people's home.

Beyond the barges was a quay where the canal workers had loaded clay for puddling the canal bed onto the repairer's barge. But nature had taken over by the time I was old enough to walk that far from home and the quay had become a tight bed of reeds and the nesting place for the old pair of mute swans that escorted an annual brood of six or seven cygnets along the waterway.

I find it interesting that this swan pair had lived through the times about which the chapters of this book have recorded and can testify to the fact that unlike the other swan pairs breeding in the area, the female or 'pen' was considerably larger than the cob, which I described in my boyhood notebook as being 'a portly bird'.

The cob was known locally as 'Joey', particularly by the Jackson family who lived at the holding situated a field's width from the canal. Vernon Jackson, a son of the family, was photographed with his mother and brothers and sisters feeding 'Joey' in 1925 and I have photographs taken thirty years later of that same swan pair, both of which succumbed to the harsh winter conditions in 1963/1964.

Like many a country wandering boy of thirty or forty years ago I experience twinges of nostalgia each time I visit an agricultural show and see such cattle breeds as the Ayrshire, Dairy Shorthorn and Blue Albion. Moreover, I have a vivid recollection of standing on the old hump-backed Gamston Bridge one hot Sunday morning and watching the Red Polled cows cooling their hocks in the shallows of the Grantham Canal.

For further recollections of winter fields and the silence with which they are synonymous, I allow my mind to take the ridge-backed lane between the villages of Strelley and Cossall, where in the November fog, the only sounds one heard was the almost inaudible splashing of water dripping from the tree branches and the 'conk conk' calls of coot establishing their feeding territories on the lake in the hollow beside Oldmoor Wood.

The Jackson family, around 1925, feeding 'Joey' the cob swan on Wollaton Canal. Balloon Woods are in the background. Joey was still breeding in 1953/1956. (Photograph: S.Jackson)

If next November, I wended my way up the footpaths in the fog all such sounds would be drowned by the perpetual roar of traffic travelling the M1 Motorway which cuts beneath the ridge-backed lane.

Thankfully, Oldmoor Wood is being preserved and managed by the Woodland Trust and pleasantly many other tracts of old woodland and marshland are similarly managed and monitored by the Nottinghamshire Naturalists Trust and other conservation groups. Not that the buildings, the manor houses, barns and dovecotes have been forgotten because we are fortunate in that few people hereabout are keen to lose their links with the past and each village, or cluster of villages, appears to have found its champions whose aims are to preserve what little remains. Thus we have now a worthy scattering of village preservation societies and their presence, it is hoped, will serve as one meaningful voice should their village boundaries become threatened by urban expansion.

Sharpening stone beside the forgotten towpath of the canal at Swansea Bridge, Trowell.

Village life was, and in some cases still is, organic, and the property developers term 'commuter haven' will never fit, even though many old cottages and gate-lodges have been converted into very comfortable and centrally heated homes that the past occupants would barely recognise.

Traditional architecture and satellite dishes are so obviously accepted into the modern village scene, while the mellowness of yesteryear that almost everyone seems to be seeking, is rediscovered as, between evening television programmes, people thumb through the pages of Edward Thomas, Flora Thompson and Laurie Lee.

Fortunately, the bell ringing tradition it still maintained and the younger generations are keen to rent derelict outbuildings as craft centres. But I admit to carrying a hatred for those vandals of both the city and countryside who force church authorities to lock the doors, although in some cases a key may be loaned from the Rectory on request.

The few, old established villagers are sometimes resentful of the 'new people' as they call them, and a few do tend to create a bad impression.

Black liner bags filled with rubbish dumped over the churchyard wall. Garages broken into and people arriving at the door with petitions drawn up in an attempt to stop a farmer driving his cattle along a lane that his family have been using for the past two or three hundred years. "Because of the smell", the 'new people' explain. As for Harold Smith, whose chapter was based largely upon his life in Cropwell Bishop, a neighbour who recognised the fact that the cottage still retained its slate roof and apple orchard commented:

"Do you know Harold, if you sold your cottage now, you'd be the richest man in the village." Harold, in recognising that the loss of his home would also mean the loss of the wild birds he so loves visiting his orchard, answered:

"No, I shouldn't. I should definitely be the poorest."

That viewpoint and those words are, I think, typical of those who have known quieter times and retained their bonds with ancestors who have lived close to the soil. Sadly, only a few such souls remain. Perhaps one or two scattered throughout a handful of villages. While others are to be found in old people's homes or being cared for by relatives.

Quiet, retiring folk. Not particularly interested in the future. But whose eyes become refuelled by the fires of childhood as they speak haltingly, yet fondly, of the old Nottinghamshire they remember.